TOEIC®テスト これだけ 直前1カ月 470点クリア

How to Prepare for the TOEIC® Test : Intermediate Course

鹿野晴夫

研究社

Copyright © 2011 by ICC
『TOEIC®テスト　これだけ　直前1カ月　470点クリア』

PRINTED IN JAPAN

はじめに

本書を手にされたみなさんへ

　本書『TOEIC®テスト　これだけ　直前1カ月　470点クリア』を手に取っていただき、誠にありがとうございます。
　ところで、みなさんが本書を手にされた理由は何でしょうか？　その理由が下記のものであれば、まさに本書はお探しの本です。

① 英語が苦手、または現在のTOEICスコアが470点未満
② TOEICテスト受験までの1カ月間で、成果を出したい
③ 通勤・通学など、移動時間を有効に使いたい

　TOEICテストに受験申し込みをしたあと、試験までの1カ月間に何をするか？　これがポイントです。多くの方は、TOEICテストの問題集で学習を始めます。確かにTOEICテストは、Part 1～Part 7に分かれていて、問題形式がそれぞれ異なりますから、それに慣れていないと、高いスコアは望めません。
　ですので、テスト前に問題形式に慣れておくことは絶対に必要です。でも、試験までの1カ月間、ただ漠然と問題集を解くだけでは、実力アップは望めません。問題を解くだけでなく、復習が必要なのです。
　しかし、1カ月間でどれほどの復習ができるでしょうか？
　1日平均3時間、月100時間以上学習できる方は別として、満足に復習できないまま、試験当日を迎えてしまう方も少なくないでしょう。本書『TOEIC®テスト　これだけ　直前1カ月　470点クリア』は、通勤・通学の時間くらいしか使えない方も、問題形式に慣れるだけでなく、実力アップがはかれるように、工夫しました。本書には、次の特長があります。

① 300点台から出発した著者のノウハウを凝縮

　私のTOEICテスト初受験は、社会人29歳の時、スコアは335点でした。最初の頃は、「470点クリア」も高い目標でした。そこから、1年で610点、2年3カ月で760点、3年半で850点になりました。900点突破には、7年かかりましたが、初受験からのスコアアップは、600点以上です。

　TOEICスコアは、350点・470点・600点と、壁を超えるように伸びていきます。「470点の壁」は、誰にでも超えられそうですが、そうでもありません。事実、企業・学校内で実施されているTOEIC IPテストの結果では、470点以下の方が60％を占めています。

　なぜ470点をクリアできない方が多いのでしょう？　それは、「どうやって学習したらいいかわからない」という人が多いからです。本書は、英語が苦手な方も、迷わず1カ月間トレーニングできるように、工夫しています。

② 1カ月間で、問題形式に慣れるだけでなく、実力アップ

　TOEICテストが測る英語力は、「スピード対応能力」です。具体的には、「速い英語が聴ける」「意味の通じる語句をすぐに選べる」「速く読める」ということです。本書は、みなさんがTOEICの問題形式に慣れつつ、このスピード対応能力も同時にアップできるように計算のうえ、編纂しました。

③ テキストで学習し、音声CDで復習できる

　クイズ形式で練習問題を解き、解答・解説を確認したあと、音声CDを利用して、通学・通勤などのあいだに効果的に学習できるように工夫しました。

　みなさんが、本書を上手に活用し、TOEICテスト受験までの1カ月間の学習を効果的に進めていただけることを願っています。

2011年3月

鹿野　晴夫

『**TOEIC® テスト　これだけ　直前１カ月　470 点クリア**』
目次

はじめに ……………………………………………………… 3

第 1 章　直前１カ月でも差がつくトレーニング法 …………… 7

第 2 章　Week 1 …………………………………………… 13

第 3 章　Week 2 …………………………………………… 49

第 4 章　Week 3 …………………………………………… 85

第 5 章　Week 4 ………………………………………… 121

第 6 章　最終チェック ………………………………… 157

効果的に学習できるように、各レッスンの CD トラック番号は前から振っていないのでご注意ください（12 ページをご覧ください）。
　各レッスンの最初のトラックで Week 1 Day 1, Week 1 Day 2, Week 1 Day 3... とナレーションが入りますが、このトラック番号は記してありません。

第1章

直前1カ月でも差がつくトレーニング法

1. 学習の進め方

1 470点クリアに必要な力を理解する

　まず、TOEICテストで470点をクリアする正答目標を確認しましょう。正答目標には、偶然に正解するものを含みます。TOEICテストは、Part 2が3択、他のパートは4択ですから、ただ勘で解答用紙にマークしても、Part 2は33%、他のパートは25%の確率で正答します。

　出題数が多く、正答目標の高いパートは、Part 2, Part 5, Part 7のシングルパッセージです。3つの合計は98問で、そのうち59問が正答目標です。ですから、TOEICテスト受験まで1カ月を切ったら、迷わずこの3つのパートのスコアアップをめざして、トレーニングを行ないましょう。

　一方、出題数の多くないパート（Part 1, Part 6）、正答目標の高くないパート（Part 3, Part 4, Part 7のダブルパッセージ）については、問題形式に慣れることをまず考えましょう。

470点クリアのための正答目標

セクション	Part	形式	問題数	正答目標
リスニング 100問 （45分間）	1	写真描写問題	10問	70%
	2	応答問題	30問	60%
	3	会話問題	30問	40%
	4	説明文問題	30問	40%
リーディング 100問 （75分間）	5	短文穴埋め問題	40問	60%
	6	長文穴埋め問題	12問	50%
	7	読解問題（シングルパッセージ）	28問	60%
		読解問題（ダブルパッセージ）	20問	35%

2 1カ月間の学習の流れ

本書を活用したTOEICテスト受験前1カ月間の学習の流れは、以下のとおりです。第2章～第5章の4章を1週間に1章のペースで進めて、受験直前に第6章を学習して、最終チェックをします。また、本書付属のCDを通勤・通学などのあいだに聞くことで、復習も効果的にできます。

章	週	テキスト学習内容	音声CD
第2章	Week 1	Day 1 会話文トレーニング	移動時間を活用して音声CDで復習
		Day 2 説明文トレーニング	
		Day 3 会話文トレーニング	
		Day 4 説明文トレーニング	
		Day 5 会話文トレーニング	
		Day 6 チェックテスト	
第3章	Week 2	Week 1同様	
第4章	Week 3		
第5章	Week 4		
第6章	受験直前	問題形式の最終チェック	

3 会話文・説明文トレーニングの英文

会話文トレーニングの英文は、Part 2（応答問題）の形式に近い問題を3問組み合わせました。Part 2は、話し手Aの短い問いかけに、話し手Bが発する4つの回答から最適なものを選ぶ問題です。本番のTOEICでは1問ずつすべて状況が異なりますが、これだと場面や状況といった周辺情報がなく、記憶に残りません。そこで本書では同じ状況を背景にした問題を3問組み合わせて、効果的にトレーニングできるようにしました。

説明文トレーニングの英文は、Part 7（読解問題）の形式に近い英文です。会話文・説明文ともに、TOEICテストで出題される日常生活とビジネスに関する話題を扱っています。リスニング・リーディング・文法・語彙を同じ英文でトレーニングすることで、音と文字の両面からスピード対応能力が強化でき、文法・語彙も自然と身に付きます。

2. トレーニングの方法

❶ 会話文・説明文トレーニングのステップ

本書でメインとなる第2章〜第4章のDay 1〜Day 5のトレーニングです。トレーニングは、以下のStep 1〜6の順で、1回のトレーニング時間は約20〜40分です。

Step	内容	目的	時間
1	リスニング問題 （Part 3, 4形式3問）	Part 3, 4の問題形式に慣れ、 Part 2の正答数アップをめざす。	2分
2	リーディング問題 （Part 7形式3問）	Part 7の問題形式に慣れ、 Part 7の正答数アップをめざす。	3分
3	文法・語彙問題 （Part 5形式5問）	Part 5の問題形式に慣れ、 Part 5の正答数アップをめざす。	2分
4	解答・解説チェック	解答・解説をチェックし、現時点での理解度を確認する。	3分
5	直読直解トレーニング	直読直解トレーニングで、リスニング・リーディング力を伸ばす。	5〜15分
6	基本構文トレーニング	基本構文トレーニングで、文法・語彙力を伸ばす。	5〜15分

❷ 直読直解トレーニングの方法 ＜基本編＞

TOEICテストでは、ナチュラルスピード（1分間に150語以上）の英文を聞き、リーディング問題を最後まで解くには1分間に150語以上読まなければなりません。速読速聴が、まず求められます。1分間に150語以上「聞いて・読む」ことができれば、TOEIC 600点以上のスコアが期待できます。ですから、470点クリアをめざす段階では、1分間125語以上、聞けて、読めることを目

標にしましょう。そのためには、うしろから訳して考えることなく、英語の語順どおりに理解しましょう。その練習が、「直読直解トレーニング」です。

　直読直解トレーニングの英文は、意味の区切りにスラッシュ（／）が入れてあり、意味の区切りごとに日本語訳を付けました。この英文を使って、区切り単位で、意味を理解する練習を行ないます。

直読直解トレーニング	1	CD（英語）を聞いて、英文を目で追う。
	2	CD（英語）を聞いて、日本語訳を目で追う。
	3	カンマ（,）、ピリオド（.）、スラッシュ（/）の単位で、英文の意味が理解できるか確認（理解できない部分は、日本語訳や語彙を参照）。

❸ 基本構文トレーニングの方法 ＜基本編＞

　TOEICテストには、空欄補充問題（Part 5, 6）もあります。文法・語彙問題ですが、30秒で解かないと、読解問題（Part 7）をやり残してしまいます。これは、「話す力」や「書く力」に通じるスピード対応能力を測る問題です。この能力を養うために、練習問題を解いたあと、問われていた文法・語彙を含んだ英文（基本構文）を使って、「基本構文トレーニング」を行ないます。

　われわれが母国語（日本語）を文法や語彙の理屈を意識しないで使えるのはどうしてでしょう？　それは、「リクツ」を考えなくても使えてしまう「リズム」を身に付けているからです。このリズムを身に付けるには、音読がいちばん。小学校の頃、毎日音読したのと一緒です。なお、電車の中などでは、小声か実際に声を出さない「口パク」でも効果があります。

基本構文トレーニング	1	1文ずつCD（日本語・英語）を聞き、英語を数回音読。
	2	10文の英語を続けて音読（数回）。
	3	テキストを縦に半分に折り、英語部分を見て意味がすぐにわかるか確認。

❹ チェックテスト

　第2章〜第4章のDay 6では、「チェックテスト」を行ないます。ここで、

Day 1〜Day 5で登場した単語50個の意味を確認します。Day 1〜Day 5のトレーニングの段階で、出てきた単語を意識して覚える必要はありません。Day 6のチェックテストで間違った単語の意味を確認し、通勤、通学の時間などを使って付属のCDでその音を聞けば、自然とインプットされるはずです。

5 第6章「最終チェック」

TOEICテストの問題形式を確認する25問の練習問題（約15分）です。第2章〜第5章のトレーニングを終えて、TOEICテスト受験直前に、問題形式の最終確認をして、本番に備えてください。

6 付属CDの活用方法

付属の音声CDは、下記のように構成されています。意識せずに、聞き流すだけで、語彙・基本構文の復習ができます。繰り返し聞きましょう。

CD音声が流れる順	収録	例
1	語句（日→英）	正気でない→ crazy
2	基本構文（日→英）	人は、運転中に信じられないことをします。People do some crazy things while driving.
3	本文（英）	People do some crazy things while driving : applying makeup, watching TV,
	設問（英）	1. Who is the speaker talking to?

（※効果的に学習できるように、各レッスンのCDトラック番号は前から順に振っていません。ご注意ください。）

何度も聞いて英文になじんできたら、発音された単語を続いて言ってみる（crazyのあとで、crazyと発音する）、基本構文の日本語を聞いたあと、英語の部分でシャドウイングしてみたり（少し遅れて、声をかぶせるようにつぶやく）、設問のあとでテキストを見ずに答えを考えるなどすれば、さらに効果的です。

第**2**章

Week 1

Week 1
今週のトレーニング

Step	内容		時間
1	リスニング問題（3問）		2分
2	リーディング問題（3問）		3分
3	文法・語彙問題（5問）		2分
4	解答・解説チェック		3分
5	直読直解トレーニング		5～15分
	①	CD（英語）を聞いて、英文を目で追う。	
	②	CD（英語）を聞いて、日本語訳を目で追う。	
	③	カンマ (,)、ピリオド (.)、スラッシュ (/) の単位で、英文の意味が理解できるか確認（理解できない部分は、日本語訳や語彙を参照）。	
6	基本構文トレーニング		5～15分
	①	1文ずつCD（日本語・英語）を聞き、英語を数回音読。	
	②	10文の英語を続けて音読（数回行なう）。	
	③	テキストを縦に半分に折るなどして日本語訳を隠し、英語部分を見て意味がすぐにわかるか確認。	

＜ワンポイント＞

まず、上記の基本的な手順に沿って、トレーニングしてください。Step 1「リスニング問題」がむずかしく感じられるかもしれません。これは、TOEIC Part 3, 4形式の問題ですから、むずかしく感じて当然です。8ページで説明したように、Part 3, 4は形式に慣れておくことが目的です。「まだできなくて当然」くらいの気持ちで挑戦してみてください。問題が解けなくても、落ち込む必要はありません。手順に沿ってトレーニングすれば、確実に実力はアップします。今日より、明日はもっとできるようになっている、と信じて、前向きに取り組みましょう。

Day 1　会話文トレーニング

Step 1　リスニング問題
CDを聞いて、問題を解こう。＜制限時間2分＞

Q1. At first, what is the man talking about?
　　(A) The size of the clothes
　　(B) The weight of the clothes
　　(C) The color of the clothes
　　(D) The price of the clothes

Q2. What does the conversation make clear?
　　(A) The man and woman live together.
　　(B) The man and woman are the same age.
　　(C) The man and woman work together.
　　(D) The man and woman come from the same town.

Q3. Where is the man going after 2:55?
　　(A) Upstairs
　　(B) Downstairs
　　(C) To the closet
　　(D) Outside

Step 2　リーディング問題

英文を読んで、問題を解こう。＜制限時間 3 分＞

M:　Should I separate the lights and the darks?
W:　What do you think, Kevin? How many times do I have to tell you? Always separate the lights from the darks.

M:　OK, they're in machines 3 and 5. What's the time?
W:　It's 2:30 ... so they'll be finished at 2:55. You going to go back down?
M:　Yeah, and I should put the sweats and towels in the dryer, right?

M:　Honey, where have you put the plastic hangers?
W:　They're in the front closet. Sorry, I moved them last week.

Q4.　What is probably true of the man and woman?
　　(A) They live together.
　　(B) They work for a laundry.
　　(C) They are mother and son.
　　(D) They work for the same company.

Q5.　In relation to the location of the speakers, where are the machines?
　　(A) In a different building
　　(B) In a lower part of the building
　　(C) In a higher part of the building
　　(D) On the same floor of the building

Q6.　What will happen at 2:55?
　　(A) The man will start the washing machines.
　　(B) The man will take the clothes out of the dryer.
　　(C) The clothes will finish drying.
　　(D) The clothes will finish washing.

Step 3 文法・語彙問題

空欄にふさわしい語句を選ぼう。 ＜制限時間2分＞

Q7. Should I _____ the lights and the darks as usual?
   (A) be separated
   (B) separate
   (C) separation
   (D) to separate

Q8. Always separate the lights _____ the darks, because the colors will run.
   (A) with
   (B) of
   (C) from
   (D) to

Q9. Where _____ put the plastic hangers?
   (A) you
   (B) have you
   (C) you have
   (D) was

Q10. How many times do I _____ tell you they can't be washed together?
   (A) must
   (B) want to
   (C) have to
   (D) should

Q11. And the shirts? I should put them in _____, right?
   (A) dryer
   (B) a dryer
   (C) the dryer
   (D) dryers

Step 4　解答・解説チェック

現時点での理解度を確認しよう。

問題文は、洗濯をする男女の会話です。

1. 正解 **(C)**。質問：「最初、男性は何について話していますか？」。答え：「洋服の色」。ヒント：Should I separate the lights and the darks?
2. 正解 **(A)**。質問：「この会話で、わかることは何ですか？」。答え：「男性と女性は、一緒に住んでいる」。ヒント：Honey, where have you put the plastic hangers?, They're in the front closet. Sorry, I moved them last week.
3. 正解 **(B)**。質問：「男性は、2時55分以降に、どこに行きますか？」。答え：「階下」。ヒント：女性の You going to go back down?, 男性の Yeah,
4. 正解 **(A)**。質問：「この男女について、正しいと思われることは何ですか？」。答え：「一緒に暮らしている」。ヒント：Q2同様。
5. 正解 **(B)**。質問：「話し手の位置から見て、洗濯機はどこにありますか？」。答え：「同じ建物の下のほう」。ヒント：You going to go back down?
6. 正解 **(D)**。質問：「2時55分に何が起こりますか？」。答え：「服の洗濯が終了する」。ヒント：they'll be finished at 2:55
7. 正解 **(B)**。助動詞 should があるので、separate（動詞・原形）を選ぶ。
8. 正解 **(C)**。separate A from B「AをBと分ける」を完成させる。
9. 正解 **(B)**。have you を選び、現在完了形の疑問文を完成させる。
10. 正解 **(C)**。do I のあとなので、have to を選ぶ。(A) は must I tell you、(D) は should I tell you となり、do は不要。
11. 正解 **(C)**。前置詞のあとの一般名詞は、通常冠詞がつく。文意から、どの乾燥機に入れるかわかっているので、the dryer を選ぶ。

Step 5　直読直解トレーニング

速読速聴力を高めよう。

（※日本語訳は、英語の原文の順序どおりに記してあります。）

M: Should I separate / the lights and the darks?
　　分けるべきですか、色の薄い物を濃い色物と？
W: What do you think, Kevin?
　　どう思いますか、ケビン？
　　How many times / do I have to tell you?
　　何回、あなたに教えなければならないのですか？
　　Always separate the lights / from the darks.
　　色の薄い物を必ず分けてください、濃い色物と。

M: OK, they're in machines 3 and 5. What's the time?
　　よし、それらは3番と5番の洗濯機の中です。何時ですか？
W: It's 2:30 ... / so they'll be finished / at 2:55.
　　今2時30分、だから終了します、2時55分に。
　　You going to go back down?
　　地下へ戻りますか？
M: Yeah, and I should put the sweats and towels / in the dryer, right?
　　ああ、そして私はスエットとタオルを入れるのですね、乾燥機に？

M: Honey, where have you put the plastic hangers?
　　ねえ、プラスチックのハンガーをどこに置きましたか？
W: They're in the front closet. Sorry, I moved them / last week.
　　前のクローゼットの中です。ごめんなさい、それを移動しました、先週。

語句

- **separate**：〜を分ける
- **darks**：濃い色物
- **finished**：終了した
- **dryer**：乾燥機
- **front**：前の
- **lights**：薄い色物
- **machine**：機械［ここでは洗濯機］
- **sweat**：スエット
- **hanger**：ハンガー
- **closet**：クローゼット

Step 6 　基本構文トレーニング
文法・語彙力を高めよう。

1	色の薄い物と濃い色物を分けるのですか？	Should I separate the lights and the darks?
2	どう思いますか？	What do you think?
3	何回教えなければならないのですか？	How many times do I have to tell you?
4	色の薄い物を濃い色物と必ず分けてください。	Always separate the lights from the darks.
5	それらは、3番と5番の洗濯機に入っています。	They're in machines 3 and 5.
6	何時ですか？	What's the time?
7	地下へ戻りますか？	You going to go back down?
8	それらを乾燥機に入れるのですね？	I should put them in the dryer, right?
9	プラスチックのハンガーをどこに置きましたか？	Where have you put the plastic hangers?
10	それらは、前のクローゼットの中です。	They're in the front closet.

Day 2 説明文トレーニング

Step 1 リスニング問題

CD を聞いて、問題を解こう。＜制限時間 2 分＞

Q1. Why does the speaker thank his audience?
 (A) For attending the presentation
 (B) For working hard at their jobs
 (C) For performing the task so well
 (D) For helping to set things up

Q2. How will people do the assigned task?
 (A) Individually
 (B) In one large group
 (C) In teams
 (D) With five members

Q3. What are the people interested in doing first?
 (A) Earning more money
 (B) Improving their skills
 (C) Getting transferred out of the sales section
 (D) Getting along better with their coworkers

Step 2 リーディング問題
英文を読んで、問題を解こう。＜制限時間3分＞

To all of you, I applaud you for taking time out of your busy schedules to attend this seminar. I hope you'll all go away empowered to become better salespeople and, most of all, better individuals. Now today, before I start, I want to shake things up a bit. You're going to split up into teams of five. Then I'm going to assign a task to each team. Let me tell you about the task itself. It's not a sales task per se, but it will show you how to market yourself. That's important to you both as an individual and as a valued member of a sales team. Now let's get started, shall we?

Q4. Who is attending the seminar?
　　(A) Individuals who now are salespeople
　　(B) Individuals who used to be salespeople
　　(C) Individuals who will become salespeople
　　(D) Individuals who want to become salespeople

Q5. How many teams will there be?
　　(A) Four
　　(B) Five
　　(C) Six
　　(D) The number is not stated.

Q6. What kind of task does each team have?
　　(A) One that is not related to selling anything
　　(B) One that shows people how to market themselves
　　(C) One that shows people how to sell a certain product
　　(D) One that shows people how to manage their busy schedules

Step 3 文法・語彙問題

空欄にふさわしい語句を選ぼう。 ＜制限時間2分＞

Q7. I want to shake things _____ a bit in order to make you think.
   (A) over
   (B) up
   (C) on
   (D) under

Q8. Before we begin, _____ me tell you about the task itself.
   (A) let
   (B) leave
   (C) permit
   (D) allow

Q9. It's not a sales task _____, but it's related to selling.
   (A) per se
   (B) per cent
   (C) personal
   (D) personally

Q10. Before starting, I'm going to _____ a task to each team.
   (A) sign
   (B) make
   (C) apply
   (D) assign

Q11. It will show you _____ to market yourself.
   (A) how
   (B) what
   (C) which
   (D) why

Step 4　解答・解説チェック

現時点での理解度を確認しよう。

問題文は、セミナーで、講師が内容の説明しているところです。

1. 正解 **(A)**。質問：「話し手は、なぜ聴衆に感謝していますか？」。答え：「プレゼンテーションに出席してくれたから」。ヒント：I applaud you for taking time out of your busy schedule to attend this seminar.
2. 正解 **(C)**。質問：「人びとは、課題をどのように行ないますか？」。答え：「チームで」。ヒント：You're going to split up into teams of five.
3. 正解 **(B)**。質問：「人びとが、最初に行ないたいと思っているのは何ですか？」。答え：「スキルの向上」。ヒント：I hope you'll all go away empowered to become better salespeople ...
4. 正解 **(A)**。質問：「セミナーに参加しているのは、どんな人たちですか？」。答え：「営業職の個人」。ヒント：I hope ... become better salespeople and... better individuals.
5. 正解 **(D)**。質問：「いくつのチームができるでしょう？」。答え：「数は述べられていない」。ヒント：チーム数は述べられていない。
6. 正解 **(B)**。質問：「各チームには、どんな課題が与えられていますか？」。答え：「自分たちを売り込む方法を示すもの」。ヒント：it will show you how to market yourself
7. 正解 **(B)**。文意から、shake things up「刺激を与える」を完成させる。
8. 正解 **(A)**。let me + 動詞「（自分が）これから〜する」を完成させる。(C)(D) は、me のあとが to tell なら可。
9. 正解 **(A)**。文意から、per se「本質的に」を選ぶ。
10. 正解 **(D)**。文意から、assign「〜を割り当てる」を選び、assign a task「課題を与える」を完成させる。(A)「〜に署名する」、(B)「〜を作る」、(C)「〜を適用する」。
11. 正解 **(A)**。how to + 動詞「〜する方法」を完成させる。

Step 5　直読直解トレーニング
速読速聴力を高めよう。
(※日本語訳は、英語の原文の順序どおりに記してあります。)

To all of you, I applaud you / for taking time / out of your busy schedules /
みなさん、ありがとうございました、時間を割いていただき、お忙しい中、
to attend this seminar. I hope / you'll all go away empowered / to become /
セミナー参加の。望みます、力を付けてお帰りいただくことを、なるための
better salespeople / and, most of all, better individuals. Now today,
より優れた営業職、そして、とりわけ、より優秀な個人に。さて本日、
before I start, I want to shake things up a bit. You're going to split up /
始める前に、少し刺激を与えたいと思います、みなさんは分かれます、
into teams of five. Then / I'm going to assign a task / to each team.
5人ずつのチームに。そのあとで、私が課題を与えます、各チームに。
Let me tell you / about the task itself. It's not a sales task per se,
説明します、課題について。それは本質的には販売の課題ではありません
but it will show you / how to market yourself. That's important to you /
しかしみなさんに示します、自分を売り込む方法を。それは重要です、
both as an individual / and as a valued member of a sales team.
個人としても、営業チームの価値ある一員としても。
Now let's get started, shall we?
では、始めましょうか。

語句			
applaud：〜を賞賛する		**attend**：〜に出席する	
empower：〜に能力を与える		**individual**：個人	
split up：分かれる		**assign**：〜を割り当てる	
task：課題		**per se**：本質的に	
market：〜を売り込む		**valued**：貴重な	

Step 6　基本構文トレーニング

文法・語彙力を高めよう。

11	お忙しい中、時間を割いていただき、ありがとうございます。	I applaud you for taking time out of your busy schedules.
12	みなさんが、力を付けてお帰りいただくことを望みます。	I hope you'll all go away empowered.
13	少し刺激を与えたいと思います。	I want to shake things up a bit.
14	みなさんは、5人ずつのチームに分かれます。	You're going to split up into teams of five.
15	私が、各チームに課題を与えます。	I'm going to assign a task to each team.
16	課題の内容について説明いたします。	Let me tell you about the task itself.
17	それは、本質的には販売の課題ではありません。	It's not a sales task per se.
18	それは、あなたに自分を売り込む方法を示すでしょう。	It will show you how to market yourself.
19	それは、個人として、あなたにとって大切です。	That's important to you as an individual.
20	では、始めましょうか。	Now let's get started, shall we?

Day 3 会話文トレーニング

Step 1 リスニング問題
CDを聞いて、問題を解こう。＜制限時間2分＞

Q1. What are the speakers talking about?
  (A) The future of yoga
  (B) The history of yoga
  (C) The difficulty of doing yoga regularly
  (D) The reason for doing yoga

Q2. What does the woman do?
  (A) She is a coach.
  (B) She is a businessperson.
  (C) She is yoga instructor.
  (D) She is a housewife.

Q3. What does the man advise the woman to do?
  (A) Continue to do yoga
  (B) Give up yoga
  (C) Find a different place to do yoga
  (D) Become a yoga instructor

Step 2　リーディング問題

英文を読んで、問題を解こう。＜制限時間3分＞

W:　Do you understand any of this?

M:　Well, actually, I'm a yoga teacher myself so, yes, I do.

W:　I still don't understand how doing yoga or meditating will help me sell more.

M:　The concept is simple. If your body and mind are in balance, your life will be, too.

W:　OK, I understand that, but I can't see the practical business application.

W:　Well, you've been helpful even though I still don't get the point of it all.

M:　You can't learn everything all at once. Be patient and take small steps first.

Q4.　What seems to be the woman's main interest?
　　(A) Yoga　　　　　　　　(B) Health
　　(C) Business　　　　　　(D) Meditation

Q5.　What is true of the man?
　　(A) He is a salesman.　　　(B) He is the woman's teacher.
　　(C) He is a supervisor at the woman's company.
　　(D) He understands the purpose of the exercises.

Q6.　What does the woman NOT understand?
　　(A) The connection between mind and body
　　(B) The connection between yoga and business
　　(C) The man's explanation of a simple concept
　　(D) The relationship between yoga and meditation

Step 3 文法・語彙問題

空欄にふさわしい語句を選ぼう。 ＜制限時間2分＞

Q7. I'm a yoga teacher _____, so it's familiar to me.
   (A) self
   (B) myself
   (C) himself
   (D) yourself

Q8. I'm sorry, but I still don't _____ the point of it all.
   (A) get
   (B) go
   (C) make
   (D) receive

Q9. You can't learn everything all _____ once, because it takes time.
   (A) the
   (B) that
   (C) at
   (D) in

Q10. I don't understand how that will help _____ sell more.
   (A) me
   (B) to me
   (C) on me
   (D) for me

Q11. I can't see the practical business _____ of these things.
   (A) apply
   (B) application
   (C) applied
   (D) to apply

Step 4　解答・解説チェック

現時点での理解度を確認しよう。

問題文は、営業成績を上げるためにヨガを行なうのは納得できないという女性と、それを説得しようとする男性の会話です。

1. 正解 **(D)**。質問：「話し手たちは、何について話していますか？」。答え：「ヨガを行なう理由」。ヒント：I still don't understand how doing yoga or meditating will help me sell more.
2. 正解 **(B)**。質問：「女性の職業は、何ですか？」。答え：「ビジネスパーソンである」。ヒント：Q1 同様。
3. 正解 **(A)**。質問：「男性は女性に、どうするようにアドバイスしていますか？」。答え：「ヨガを続ける」。ヒント：Be patient and take small steps first.
4. 正解 **(C)**。質問：「女性がいちばん関心のあるのは、何だと思われますか？」。答え：「ビジネス」。ヒント：Q1 同様。
5. 正解 **(D)**。質問：「男性に関して、正しい記述はどれですか？」。答え：「エクササイズの目的を理解している」。ヒント：I'm a yoga teacher myself so, yes, I do.
6. 正解 **(B)**。質問：「女性が理解していないことは、何ですか？」。答え：「ヨガとビジネスの関連性」。ヒント：Q1 同様。
7. 正解 **(B)**。文意から、myself を選び、「自分自身がヨガの講師である」ことを強調する文を完成させる。
8. 正解 **(A)**。文意から、get the point「要点をつかむ」を完成させる。
9. 正解 **(C)**。文意から、at once「一度に」の強調 all at once を完成させる。
10. 正解 **(A)**。me を選び、help +（人）+（to）+ 動詞（原形）「（人）が〜するのに役立つ」にする。
11. 正解 **(B)**。前置詞 of が続いているので、名詞 application「応用（すること）」を選び、複合名詞 business application「ビジネスへの応用」を完成させる。

Step 5　直読直解トレーニング

速読速聴力を高めよう。

（※日本語訳は、英語の原文の順序どおりに記してあります。）

W: Do you understand any of this?
　　理解できますか、これが少しでも？

M: Well, actually, I'm a yoga teacher myself so, yes, I do.
　　まあ、実は、私自身がヨガの講師なので、はい、できます。

W: I still don't understand / how doing yoga or meditating /
　　私は、まだ理解できません、どうしてヨガや瞑想をすることが、
　　will help me sell more.
　　私が売上を伸ばすことに役立つのか。

M: The concept is simple.
　　考え方は単純です。
　　If your body and mind are in balance, your life will be, too.
　　身体と心のバランスが取れていれば、生活もそうなります。

W: OK, I understand that, but I can't see /
　　はい、それは理解できます、しかしわかりません、
　　the practical business application.
　　ビジネスへの実践的な応用が。

W: Well, you've been helpful / even though I still don't get /
　　さて、助かりました、まだ私は理解できませんが、
　　the point of it all.
　　それのすべての点を。

M: You can't learn everything all at once.
　　一度にすべてを学ぶことはできません。
　　Be patient and take small steps first.
　　忍耐強く、まずは小さな一歩を。

---

actually：実のところ　**meditate**：瞑想する　**concept**：考え方　**mind**：心
balance：バランス　**practical**：実践的な　**application**：応用　**helpful**：役に立つ
at once：一度に　**patient**：忍耐強い

Step 6 基本構文トレーニング

文法・語彙力を高めよう。

21	これが少しでも理解できますか？	Do you understand any of this?
22	私自身、ヨガの講師です。	I'm a yoga teacher myself.
23	それが、どうして私が売上を増やすことに役立つのか理解できません。	I don't understand how that will help me sell more.
24	考え方は単純です。	The concept is simple.
25	あなたは、身体と心のバランスが取れています。	Your body and mind are in balance.
26	ビジネスへの実践的な応用がわかりません。	I can't see the practical business application.
27	助かりました。	You've been helpful.
28	まだ、それのすべての点は理解できません。	I still don't get the point of it all.
29	一度にすべてを学ぶことはできません。	You can't learn everything all at once.
30	辛抱強く、まずは小さな一歩から。	Be patient and take small steps first.

Day 4 説明文トレーニング

Step 1 リスニング問題
CD を聞いて、問題を解こう。＜制限時間2分＞

Q1. What does the speaker thank his listeners for?
　　(A) Fixing the slide projector
　　(B) Coming out in the bad weather
　　(C) Arriving early
　　(D) Waiting quietly

Q2. What do the slides show?
　　(A) Stores and shops
　　(B) The speaker's colleagues
　　(C) Vacation sites
　　(D) The speaker's relatives

Q3. What does the speaker want to do?
　　(A) Tear down the Chinese restaurant and the hair salon
　　(B) Copy the development along Bermont Road
　　(C) Design something different
　　(D) Put together an area that is a mishmash of ideas

Step 2　リーディング問題
英文を読んで、問題を解こう。＜制限時間3分＞

Thank you for your patience. I think we have the slide projector up and running now. Now, I'll draw your attention to this area here. As you notice, there seems to be a lot of development along Bermont Road, but it's all haphazard. I'll go through these next few slides so you can see what I mean. We have a Fotomat, an art gallery, a rental DVD shop, a sort of mini-mall, a Chinese restaurant right next to a hair salon, and so on. All these businesses are fine on their own, but together it's just a mishmash of usages and building design. This is why we want to try something new this time around.

Q4. What was the speaker's problem before this passage began?
   (A) The equipment was not working.
   (B) The slides were not organized well.
   (C) The other speaker had not arrived yet.
   (D) The people in the audience were not listening to him.

Q5. How does the speaker describe the businesses along Bermont Road now?
   (A) An unplanned mixture
   (B) A shopping center with an overall design
   (C) Small shops selling the same kinds of goods
   (D) Mostly business offices and medical services

Q6. Why is the speaker making this presentation?
   (A) To get more customers
   (B) To suggest new ideas for development
   (C) To invite new businesses to Bermont Road
   (D) To explain why the old buildings will be destroyed

Step 3 文法・語彙問題

空欄にふさわしい語句を選ぼう。 ＜制限時間2分＞

Q7. Thank you for your _____ , Ladies and Gentlemen.
- (A) patient
- (B) patients
- (C) patiently
- (D) patience

Q8. There seems to be _____ development along Bermont Road.
- (A) lots
- (B) a lot of
- (D) the lots of
- (C) a lot

Q9. This is why we want to try _____ with this development plan.
- (A) something new
- (B) some news
- (C) new something
- (D) anything new

Q10. We have the slide projector up and _____ now, so we can start.
- (A) run
- (B) go
- (C) running
- (D) going

Q11. All these businesses are fine on _____ own, but together, there's no pattern.
- (A) they
- (B) their
- (C) them
- (D) theirs

Step 4　解答・解説チェック

現時点での理解度を確認しよう。

問題文は、地元の開発に関する提案のプレゼンです。

1. 正解 **(D)**。質問：「話し手は、何を聴衆に感謝していますか？」。答え：「忍耐強く待っていたこと」。ヒント：Thank you for your patience.
2. 正解 **(A)**。質問：「スライドは、何を示していますか？」。答え：「店舗」。ヒント：We have a Fotomat, an art gallery, a rental DVD shop, a sort of mini-mall など。
3. 正解 **(C)**。質問：「話し手は、何をしたいと思っていますか？」。答え：「他とは違う設計」。ヒント：we want to try something new
4. 正解 **(A)**。質問：「この話が始まる前の、話し手の問題は何でしたか？」。答え：「機器が作動していなかった」。ヒント：I think we have the slide projector up and running now.
5. 正解 **(A)**。質問：「現在のバーモント通り沿いの店舗を、話し手はどのように描写していますか？」。答え：「無計画な混合」。ヒント：it's just a mishmash of usages and building design
6. 正解 **(B)**。質問：「話し手はなぜ、このプレゼンをしていますか？」。答え：「開発のための新しいアイデアを提案するため」。ヒント：we want to try something new
7. 正解 **(D)**。patience「忍耐」を選び、「お待たせいたしました」を完成させる。
8. 正解 **(B)**。development「開発」は、不可算名詞。数・量ともに「多い」を表わす a lot of を選ぶ。
9. 正解 **(A)**。文意から、something new「何か新しいもの」を選ぶ。(C) の語順はない。
10. 正解 **(C)**。have +（物）+ up and running「（物）が作動している」を完成させる。
11. 正解 **(B)**。文意から、on their own「それ自体（単独では）」を完成させる。

Step 5 　直読直解トレーニング
速読速聴力を高めよう。
(※日本語訳は、英語の原文の順序どおりに記してあります。)

Thank you for your patience. I think / we have the slide projector /
お待たせいたしました。思います、スライド・プロジェクターの、
up and running now. Now, I'll draw your attention / to this area here.
用意ができていると。では、ご注目いただきます、こちらのこの地域に。
As you notice, there seems to be a lot of development /
お気づきのとおり、多くの開発が行なわれているようです、
along Bermont Road, but it's all haphazard.
バーモント通り沿いに、しかしそれはまったく無計画です。
I'll go through these next few slides /
次の数枚のスライドを説明します、
so you can see what I mean. We have a Fotomat, an art gallery,
私の言っていることがおわかりいただける。フォトマット、アートギャラリー、
a rental DVD shop, a sort of mini-mall, a Chinese restaurant /
レンタルDVDショップ、小型ショッピングモールの類、中華料理店、
right next to a hair salon, and so on. All these businesses are fine /
美容室のすぐ隣に、などがあります。これらすべての店舗は結構です、
on their own, but together / it's just a mishmash /
個別には、でも総体的に見ると、寄せ集めにすぎません、
of usages and building design. This is why / we want to try something new /
既存のものと、建築デザインの。ですから、何か新しいものを試したいのです、
this time around.
今回は。

語句		
up and running：作動している		**attention**：注目
notice：気づく		**development**：開発
haphazard：無計画の		**go through**：〜を論ずる
and so on：〜など		**mishmash**：寄せ集め
usage：慣習		**this time around**：今回は

Step 6　基本構文トレーニング

文法・語彙力を高めよう。

31	お待たせいたしました。	Thank you for your patience.
32	スライド・プロジェクターの用意ができています。	We have the slide projector up and running now.
33	こちらのこの地域にご注目ください。	I'll draw your attention to this area here.
34	たくさんの開発が行なわれているようです。	There seems to be a lot of development.
35	それは、まったく無計画です。	It's all haphazard.
36	次の数枚のスライドを説明します。	I'll go through these next few slides.
37	私の言っていることがおわかりいただけます。	You can see what I mean.
38	これらすべての店舗は、個別には結構です。	All these businesses are fine on their own.
39	既存のものと建築デザインの寄せ集めにすぎません。	It's just a mishmash of usages and building design.
40	ですから、何か新しいものを試したいのです。	This is why we want to try something new.

Week 1

Day 5 会話文トレーニング

Step 1 リスニング問題
CD を聞いて、問題を解こう。＜制限時間 2 分＞

Q1. Who is the woman?
　　(A) A bank employee
　　(B) A customer at a bank
　　(C) Someone who wants a new passport
　　(D) Someone who wants a safety deposit box

Q2. When will the man have a safety deposit box?
　　(A) Tomorrow
　　(B) Later in the day
　　(C) Sometime in the future
　　(D) As soon as he gets a driver's license

Q3. Which will happen first?
　　(A) The man will get his safety deposit box.
　　(B) The man will bring in a copy of a page from his passport.
　　(C) The man will return to the bank.
　　(D) The man will sign a paper.

Step 2　リーディング問題

英文を読んで、問題を解こう。＜制限時間 3 分＞

W: What can I do for you today, Mr. Lefferts?
M: Well, remember when I was in here before? I was wondering about opening a safety deposit box.

W: It's fairly simple, you see. Just sign the authorization form here. And I'll need to make a photocopy of your driver's license.
M: Actually, I don't have one. I don't drive.
W: OK, we'll need some kind of photo ID. Do you have a passport?

W: Fine. Just bring in a copy of the photo page of your passport and I'll send all that in immediately.
M: Right. I'll drop that by tomorrow.

Q4. Who is Mr. Lefferts?
　(A) A driver　　　　　　(B) A customer
　(C) A safety officer　　　(D) A bank employee

Q5. Why does the woman want to see Mr. Lefferts' passport?
　(A) Because he is a foreigner
　(B) Because he is going to take a trip
　(C) Because he lost his driver's license
　(D) Because she needs to see a photo ID

Q6. What will Mr. Lefferts do on the day after this conversation?
　(A) Come to the bank again
　(B) Make a copy of his photograph
　(C) Send his passport to the woman
　(D) Deposit some money in the bank

Step 3　文法・語彙問題

空欄にふさわしい語句を選ぼう。　＜制限時間2分＞

Q7. Just _____ the authorization form here and then we're finished.
- (A) to sign
- (B) sign
- (C) sign up
- (D) signature

Q8. We'll need some kind of photo _____ if you don't have a driver's license.
- (A) DI
- (B) OD
- (C) DO
- (D) ID

Q9. I'll send all that in _____, no later than tomorrow.
- (A) immediate
- (B) medium
- (C) immediately
- (D) medium time

Q10. I was _____ about opening a safety deposit box here at the bank.
- (A) wondered
- (B) wondering
- (C) wonder
- (D) wonderful

Q11. I'll need to make a photocopy of your _____ license.
- (A) driving
- (B) drive
- (C) driver's
- (D) drivers

Step 4　解答・解説チェック

現時点での理解度を確認しよう。

問題文は、貸金庫を利用しようとする客と銀行員の会話です。

1. 正解 **(A)**。質問：「女性は、どんな人ですか？」。答え：「銀行員」。ヒント：I was wondering about opening a safety box.
2. 正解 **(C)**。質問：「男性が貸金庫を借りるのは、いつですか？」。答え：「少し先」。ヒント：I'll drop that by tomorrow. ただし、明日から使用できるかどうかは不明なので（C）が正解。
3. 正解 **(D)**。質問：「最初に起こるのは、何ですか？」。答え：「男性が、書類に署名をする」。ヒント：Just sign the authorization form here.
4. 正解 **(B)**。質問：「レファーツ氏は、どんな人ですか？」。答え：「顧客」。ヒント：What can I do for you today, Mr. Lefferts?
5. 正解 **(D)**。質問：「女性は、なぜレファーツ氏のパスポートを見たいのですか？」。答え：「写真付き身分証明書が必要だから」。ヒント：we'll need some kind of photo ID
6. 正解 **(A)**。質問：「この会話が行なわれた翌日、レファーツ氏は何をしますか？」。答え：「もう一度銀行に来る」。ヒント：I'll drop that by tomorrow.
7. 正解 **(B)**。文意から、sign「～に署名する」（動詞）を選ぶ。(C)「登録する」（動詞）。(D)「署名」（名詞）。
8. 正解 **(D)**。文意から、ID「身分証明書」を選び、photo ID「写真付き身分証明書」を完成させる。
9. 正解 **(C)**。文意から、動詞 send を修飾する副詞 immediately「すぐに」を選ぶ。(A)「即座の」（形容詞）、(B)「中間」（名詞）。
10. 正解 **(B)**。I was wondering about「～しようかと思っていた」を完成させる。
11. 正解 **(C)**。文意から、driver's license「運転免許証」を完成させる。

Step 5　直読直解トレーニング
速読速聴力を高めよう。

(※日本語訳は、英語の原文の順序どおりに記してあります。)

W: What can I do for you today, Mr. Lefferts?
本日は、どのようなご用件ですかレファーツさん？

M: Well, remember when I was in here before?
ええと、以前に私がここに来たのを覚えていますか？
I was wondering / about opening a safety deposit box.
思っていたのですが、貸金庫を利用しようと。

W: It's fairly simple, you see. Just sign the authorization form here.
それは、比較的簡単ですよ。こちらの承諾書に、ご署名ください。
And I'll need to / a make a photocopy / of your driver's license.
それと、必要があります、コピーをさせていただく、運転免許証の。

M: Actually, I don't have one. I don't drive.
実は、持っていないのです。私は運転しません。

W: OK, we'll need some kind of photo ID.
では、何か写真付きの身分証明書が必要です。
Do you have a passport?
パスポートをお持ちですか？

W: Fine. Just bring in a copy / of the photo page of your passport /
結構です。コピーをお持ちください、パスポートの写真ページの、
and I'll send all that in / immediately.
そうすれば、すべてを手続きいたします、すぐに。

M: Right. I'll drop that by / tomorrow.
わかりました。それを届けます、明日。

語句

safety deposit box：貸金庫　**fairly**：いくぶん　**sign**：〜に署名する
authorization：承諾　**photocopy**：コピー　**ID**：身分証明書
bring in：〜を持ってくる　**send in**：〜の手続きをする
immediately：ただちに　**drop by**：〜を届ける

Step 6　基本構文トレーニング
文法・語彙力を高めよう。

41	本日は、どのようなご用件でしょう？	What can I do for you today?
42	貸金庫を利用しようと思っていたのですが。	I was wondering about opening a safety deposit box.
43	それは、比較的簡単ですよ。	It's fairly simple, you see.
44	こちらの承諾書に、ご署名ください。	Just sign the authorization form here.
45	運転免許証のコピーをさせていただく必要があります。	I'll need to make a photocopy of your driver's license.
46	私は、運転しません。	I don't drive.
47	何か写真付きの身分証明書が必要です。	We'll need some kind of photo ID.
48	パスポートのコピーをお持ちください。	Just bring in a copy of your passport.
49	すぐに、すべてを手続きいたします。	I'll send all that in immediately.
50	明日、それを届けます。	I'll drop that by tomorrow.

Day 6 チェックテスト

ふさわしい語句の意味を選ぼう。　＜制限時間５分＞

1. separate：(A) 〜を引っ張る　(B) 〜を押す　(C) 〜を分ける
2. lights：(A) 薄い色物　(B) 右側　(C) 照明係
3. darks：(A) アヒル　(B) 濃い色物　(C) 暗闇
4. machine：(A) 機械　(B) 適合　(C) 行進
5. finished：(A) 最後の　(B) 終了した　(C) うしろ向きに
6. sweat：(A) 甘い　(B) スエット　(C) 滑らかな
7. dryer：(A) 乾燥機　(B) クリーニング店　(C) 柔軟剤
8. hanger：(A) ハンガー　(B) 崖　(C) 空腹
9. front：(A) 自由な　(B) うしろの　(C) 前の
10. closet：(A) 閉じた　(B) もっとも近い　(C) クローゼット

11. applaud：(A) 〜を賞賛する　(B) 〜を非難する　(C) 大声を出す
12. attend：(A) 〜と一致する　(B) 〜に同意する　(C) 〜に出席する
13. empower：(A) 〜に電力を供給する　(B) 〜に能力を与える
　　　　　　(C) 〜と力を合わせる
14. individual：(A) ビジュアルの　(B) 個人　(C) 分配
15. split up：(A) 分かれる　(B) つばを吐く　(C) 上に向かって切る
16. assign：(A) 〜に署名する　(B) 〜を割り当てる　(C) 看板を掲げる
17. task：(A) 持っていく　(B) 課題　(C) 税金
18. per se：(A) 本質的に　(B) それなりに　(C) その場合
19. market：(A) 〜をマークする　(B) 市場に行く　(C) 〜を売り込む
20. valued：(A) 過剰な　(B) お得な　(C) 貴重な

21. actually：(A) 偶然にも　(B) 実のところ　(C) 仮に
22. meditate：(A) 薬を飲む　(B) 瞑想する　(C) 貢献する
23. concept：(A) 考え方　(B) 集中　(C) コンセント
24. mind：(A) 心　(B) 内臓　(C) 心臓
25. balance：(A) 重さ　(B) 平均的な　(C) バランス

26. practical：(A) プラスチック製の　(B) 実践的な　(C) 練習用の
27. application：(A) 基本　(B) 理論　(C) 応用
28. helpful：(A) 助けが必要な　(B) 助けられた　(C) 役に立つ
29. at once：(A) 一度に　(B) 一度だけ　(C) 珍しく
30. patient：(A) 病気の　(B) 特許の　(C) 忍耐強い

31. up and running：(A) 起きて走る　(B) 上り坂を走る
　　　　　　　　　　(C) 作動している
32. attention：(A) 注目　(B) 注文　(C) 注意点
33. notice：(A) 異なる　(B) 気づく　(C) メモを取る
34. development：(A) 開発　(B) 研究　(C) 事業
35. haphazard：(A) 防災上の　(B) 緊急時の　(C) 無計画の
36. go through：(A) 〜に物を投げる　(B) 〜を論ずる　(C) 〜を軽蔑する
37. and so on：(A) それから　(B) 〜など　(C) 始める
38. mishmash：(A) 攻撃　(B) 分散　(C) 寄せ集め
39. usage：(A) 慣習　(B) ソーセージ　(C) 役に立つ
40. this time around：(A) 最近は　(B) 今回は　(C) 次回は

41. safety deposit box：(A) 貸金庫　(B) 金庫　(C) 保証金
42. fairly：(A) 妖精　(B) 素早く　(C) いくぶん
43. sign：(A) 歌う　(B) ため息をつく　(C) 〜に署名する
44. authorization：(A) 命令　(B) 指示　(C) 承諾
45. photocopy：(A) コピー　(B) 写真　(C) 印刷物
46. ID：(A) 借用証　(B) 小切手　(C) 身分証明書
47. bring in：(A) 〜をかつぐ　(B) 〜を運び出す　(C) 〜を持ってくる
48. send in：(A) 〜を投げ込む　(B) 〜の手続きをする
　　　　　　(C) 〜の手助けをする
49. immediately：(A) わずかに　(B) ただちに　(C) やがて
50. drop by：(A) 〜を届ける　(B) 〜を落とす　(C) 〜を壊す

チェックテスト解答

1. **(C)**	2. **(A)**	3. **(B)**	4. **(A)**	5. **(B)**
6. **(B)**	7. **(A)**	8. **(A)**	9. **(C)**	10. **(C)**
11. **(A)**	12. **(C)**	13. **(B)**	14. **(B)**	15. **(A)**
16. **(B)**	17. **(B)**	18. **(A)**	19. **(C)**	20. **(C)**
21. **(B)**	22. **(B)**	23. **(A)**	24. **(A)**	25. **(C)**
26. **(B)**	27. **(C)**	28. **(C)**	29. **(A)**	30. **(C)**
31. **(C)**	32. **(A)**	33. **(B)**	34. **(A)**	35. **(C)**
36. **(B)**	37. **(B)**	38. **(C)**	39. **(A)**	40. **(B)**
41. **(A)**	42. **(C)**	43. **(C)**	44. **(C)**	45. **(A)**
46. **(C)**	47. **(C)**	48. **(B)**	49. **(B)**	50. **(A)**

<ワンポイント>

　第1週のトレーニングはいかがでしたか？　やはり、Step 1「リスニング問題」がむずかしく感じられたでしょうか？　繰り返しになりますが、Part 3, 4の問題形式に慣れることが目的ですから、間違っても気にしないことです。

　問題形式に慣れるという点では、正答できたかどうかより、設問（Q1～Q6）を素早く理解できたことのほうが大事です。Part 3, 4, 7の設問は、合計108問。設問の意味がすぐにわからなければ、焦って間違うか（Part 3, 4）、解答時間が足りなくなります（Part 7）。

　ですから、Step 4「解答・解説チェック」の際は、設問の意味を正しく理解できていたかを確認することが大事です（選択肢は、正解の意味だけ確認すれば大丈夫です）。

　また、Step 5～6のトレーニングはいかがでしたか？「トレーニング内容が少し物足りない」「もっとトレーニングしたい」と感じた方には、Week 2（50ページ）、Week 3（86ページ）、Week 4（122ページ）に応用トレーニングを紹介していますので、チャレンジしてみてください。

第**3**章

Week 2

Week 2
今週のトレーニング

Day 1～ Day 5 のトレーニング			
Step	内容		時間
1	リスニング問題（3問）		2分
2	リーディング問題（3問）		3分
3	文法・語彙問題（5問）		2分
4	解答・解説チェック		3分
5	直読直解トレーニング		5～15分
	①	CD（英語）を聞いて、英文を目で追う。	
	②	CD（英語）を聞いて、日本語訳を目で追う。	
	③	カンマ (,)、ピリオド (.)、スラッシュ (/) の単位で、英文の意味が理解できるか確認（理解できない部分は、日本語訳や語彙を参照）。	
6	基本構文トレーニング		5～15分
	①	1文ずつCD（日本語・英語）を聞き、英語を数回音読。	
	②	10文の英語を続けて音読（数回行なう）。	
	③	テキストを縦に半分に折るなどして日本語訳を隠し、英語部分を見て意味がすぐにわかるか確認。	
	④	応用トレーニング「ルックアップ＆セイ」	

<ワンポイント>

　先週のトレーニングはいかがでしたか？　少し物足りないと感じた方は、Step 6の④「応用トレーニング」として、以下を追加学習してください。テキストを見ないで基本構文を話す練習で、さらに学習効果が期待できます。

ルックアップ＆セイ	英文を音読したあと、顔を上げて（英文を見ずに）、英文を話す（小声か口パクでもOK）。言えなかった英文は何度か音読し、再チャレンジしてください。

Week 2

Day 1 会話文トレーニング

Step 1 リスニング問題
CD を聞いて、問題を解こう。＜制限時間2分＞

Q1. What is true of both speakers?
    (A) They love the Beatles.
    (B) They like music.
    (C) They saw the Rolling Stones on tour last year.
    (D) They play musical instruments.

Q2. How are the man's and woman's tastes in music?
    (A) He likes newer groups than she does.
    (B) He likes older groups than she does.
    (C) They both like old groups.
    (D) They both like new groups.

Q3. Which of the following describes the man?
    (A) He is somewhat bored.
    (B) He is a little angry.
    (C) He is a bit sarcastic.
    (D) He is rather intellectual.

Step 2　リーディング問題

英文を読んで、問題を解こう。＜制限時間３分＞

M:　So, are you into music, Stacey?
W:　Oh, yeah, I love the Beatles! They're my favorite group.

M:　The Beatles? You know, rock music did not stop in 1970. What about today's bands?
W:　Oh, I love the Rolling Stones. I just saw them on tour last year.
M:　OK, sure. Let me rephrase that: Do you like any bands from the past decade?

M:　It looks like I'm going to have to burn you a couple of CDs to update your musical tastes.
W:　That'll be cool! I really want to hear this band called the Raveonettes you just told me about.

Q4.　How many music groups are named in the dialogue?
　　　(A) Two　　　　　　　　(B) Three
　　　(C) Four　　　　　　　　(D) Many

Q5.　What does the man think about the woman's musical tastes?
　　　(A) They are bad.　　　　(B) They are good.
　　　(C) They are funny.　　　(D) They are out of date.

Q6.　What is the man going to do for the woman?
　　　(A) Take her to a Raveonettes concert
　　　(B) Give her some new music on CDs
　　　(C) Take her to a Rolling Stones concert
　　　(D) Buy some recordings for her on CDs

Step 3　文法・語彙問題

空欄にふさわしい語句を選ぼう。　＜制限時間２分＞

Q7. I just saw them _____ tour last year and they were great.
　　(A) on
　　(B) in
　　(C) to
　　(D) of

Q8. _____ me rephrase that so you can understand it more easily.
　　(A) Let
　　(B) Let's
　　(C) Letting
　　(D) Lets

Q9. I want _____ this band called the Raveonettes.
　　(A) hearing
　　(B) to hear
　　(C) hear about
　　(D) hear

Q10. Do you like _____ bands from the past decade, or only old music?
　　(A) any of
　　(B) anyone
　　(C) any
　　(D) which

Q11. I'm going to have _____ you a couple of CDs of new music on them.
　　(A) to burn
　　(B) burn
　　(C) to be burned
　　(D) burning

Step 4　解答・解説チェック

現時点での理解度を確認しよう。

問題文は、音楽の好みについて話している男女の会話です。

1. 正解 **(B)**。質問:「2人の話し手に関して、正しいことは何ですか？」。答え:「音楽が好き」。ヒント:It looks like I'm going to have to burn you a couple of CDs
2. 正解 **(A)**。質問:「男性と女性の音楽の好みは、どうですか？」。答え:「男性は、女性より新しいグループを好む」。ヒント:burn you a couple of CDs to update your musical tastes.
3. 正解 **(C)**。質問:「男性について説明しているのは、次のどれですか？」。答え:「少々皮肉っぽい」。ヒント:You know, rock music did not stop in 1970.
4. 正解 **(B)**。質問:「会話では、いくつの音楽グループが述べられていますか？」。答え:「3つ」。ヒント:the Beatles, the Rolling Stones, the Raveonettes
5. 正解 **(D)**。質問:「男性は、女性の音楽の好みについてどう思っていますか？」。答え:「流行遅れ」。ヒント:You know, rock music did not stop in 1970.
6. 正解 **(B)**。質問:「男性は、女性に何をしてあげますか？」。答え:「新しい音楽のCDをあげる」。ヒント:I'm going to have to burn you a couple of CDs
7. 正解 **(A)**。on tour「ツアー（演奏旅行）中」を完成させる。
8. 正解 **(A)**。Let me + 動詞「（私が）～します」を完成させる。
9. 正解 **(B)**。to hear を選び、want to + 動詞「～したい」を完成させる。
10. 正解 **(C)**。「(0を含む) いくつか」を尋ねる any を選ぶ。
11. 正解 **(A)**。「あなたにCDを焼いてあげなければならない」という文意から、to burn を選び、have to + 動詞「～しなければならない」を完成させる。

Step 5　直読直解トレーニング

速読速聴力を高めよう。

(※日本語訳は、英語の原文の順序どおりに記してあります。)

M: So, are you into music, Stacey?
　　では、音楽が好きですか、ステーシー？

W: Oh, yeah, I love the Beatles! They're my favorite group.
　　ええ、そう、ビートルズに夢中です！　彼らはお気に入りのグループです。

M: The Beatles? You know, rock music did not stop /
　　ビートルズ？　あのね、ロック・ミュージックは終わっていません、
　　in 1970. What about today's bands?
　　1970年で。今のバンドはどうですか？

W: Oh, I love the Rolling Stones.
　　ええ、ローリング・ストーンズが大好きです。
　　I just saw them / on tour last year.
　　彼らを折よく見ました、去年ツアー中の。

M: OK, sure. Let me rephrase that:
　　はいはい。　言い直させてください。
　　Do you like / any bands from the past decade?
　　好きですか、ここ10年のバンドのどれかを？

M: It looks like / I'm going to have to burn you /
　　どうやら、あなたに焼いてあげなければならないようです、
　　a couple of CDs / to update your musical tastes.
　　CDを何枚か、あなたの音楽の嗜好を新しくするために。

W: That'll be cool! I really want to hear this band /
　　それは、最高！このバンドをぜひ聞きたいです、
　　called the Raveonettes / you just told me about.
　　レヴォネッツという、あなたが今話してくれた。

語句

be into：〜に夢中　**favorite**：お気に入りの　**on tour**：ツアー中
rephrase：〜を言い換える　**decade**：10年間　**burn**：〜を焼く
update：〜を更新する　**musical**：音楽の　**taste**：嗜好　**cool**：すばらしい

Step 6　基本構文トレーニング

文法・語彙力を高めよう。

51	音楽が好きですか、ステーシー？	Are you into music, Stacey?
52	彼らは、私のいちばんお気に入りのグループです。	They're my favorite group.
53	ロック・ミュージックは1970年で終わってはいません。	Rock music did not stop in 1970.
54	今のバンドはどうですか？	What about today's bands?
55	去年、ツアー中の彼らを、折よく見ました。	I just saw them on tour last year.
56	それを、言い直します。	Let me rephrase that.
57	ここ10年のバンドのどれかを好きですか？	Do you like any bands from the past decade?
58	あなたにCDを何枚か焼いてあげなければならないようです。	I'm going to have to burn you a couple of CDs.
59	それは、最高！	That'll be cool!
60	このレヴォネッツというバンドを聞きたいです。	I want to hear this band called the Raveonettes.

Day 2 説明文トレーニング

Step 1 リスニング問題
CD を聞いて、問題を解こう。＜制限時間 2 分＞

Q1. Who is this message directed toward?
- (A) Parents
- (B) Children
- (C) Teachers
- (D) Neighbors

Q2. What kind of costume is recommended?
- (A) One that is funny to look at
- (B) One that is very scary
- (C) One that can be seen easily
- (D) One that can be put on and taken quickly

Q3. Which Halloween activity does the speaker mention?
- (A) Carving faces into pumpkins
- (B) Eating candy apples
- (C) Visiting haunted houses
- (D) Lighting fireworks

Step 2 リーディング問題

英文を読んで、問題を解こう。＜制限時間3分＞

It's that time of year again. Time to go trick-or-treating. Make your Halloween a safe one this year. Remember to always go trick-or-treating with an adult or a teenaged sibling. Wear a bright costume, or have someone in your group carry a flashlight so you can be seen by cars on the road. Stick to neighborhoods and houses you know. Also, remember fireworks can be dangerous. Light them only in the presence of a parent or other adult. If you just keep these few safety tips in mind, you'll have a safe and happy Halloween.

Q4. What does the passage do?
- (A) Give a short history of Halloween customs
- (B) Suggest ways for having a good Halloween
- (C) Recommend ways to make Halloween costumes at home
- (D) Ask people to share their Halloween experiences

Q5. According to the message, what should NOT be done?
- (A) Wearing costumes
- (B) Lighting fireworks
- (C) Walking with siblings
- (D) Going to unfamiliar areas

Q6. What is the main point of the passage?
- (A) Have a safe Halloween.
- (B) Be careful with fireworks.
- (C) Go trick-or-treating with an adult.
- (D) Be polite when visiting neighbors.

Step 3 文法・語彙問題

空欄にふさわしい語句を選ぼう。 ＜制限時間2分＞

Q7. It's Halloween, and it's time _____ trick-or-treating.
　　(A) about going
　　(B) of going
　　(C) to go
　　(D) will go

Q8. You should stick _____ neighborhoods and houses you know.
　　(A) at
　　(B) on
　　(C) to
　　(D) of

Q9. If you have fireworks, light them only in the _____ of a parent or other adult.
　　(A) presence　　　　(B) preview
　　(C) presents　　　　(D) pressure

Q10. Be sure to make your Halloween a _____ one this year.
　　(A) safe
　　(B) safely
　　(C) safety
　　(D) safest

Q11. That way, you can be _____ by cars on the road.
　　(A) see
　　(B) seeing
　　(C) seen
　　(D) saw

Step 4　解答・解説チェック

現時点での理解度を確認しよう。

問題文は、ハロウィーンを安全で楽しいものにするための注意事項です。

1. 正解 **(B)**。質問：「このメッセージは、誰に向けられたものですか？」。答え：「子供たち」。ヒント：Remember to ... with an adult or a teenaged sibling.
2. 正解 **(C)**。質問：「どのような衣装が勧められていますか？」。答え：「目に留まりやすいもの」。ヒント：Wear a bright costume.
3. 正解 **(D)**。質問：「話し手が述べているハロウィーンでの行為は、どれですか？」。答え：「花火を点火する」。ヒント：Light them only in the presence of a parent
4. 正解 **(B)**。質問：「何のための文書ですか？」。答え：「ハロウィーンを楽しく過ごすための提案」。ヒント：If you just keep these few safety tips in mind, you'll have a safe and happy Halloween.
5. 正解 **(D)**。質問：「メッセージによると、やってはいけないことは何ですか？」。答え：「不慣れな場所に行くこと」。ヒント：Stick to neighborhoods and houses you know.
6. 正解 **(A)**。質問：「この文書のポイントは何ですか？」。答え：「安全なハロウィーンを過ごすこと」。ヒント：If you just keep these few safety tips in mind, you'll have a safe and happy Halloween.
7. 正解 **(C)**。to go を選び、time to + 動詞「～（をするため）の時期」を完成させる。
8. 正解 **(C)**。stick to「～に固執する」を完成させる。
9. 正解 **(A)**。文意から、in the presence of +（人・物）「（人・物）がその場に存在する状態で」を完成させる。
10. 正解 **(A)**。形容詞 safe を選び、safe one「安全なもの」を完成させる。
11. 正解 **(C)**。文意から、受動態 be seen「見られる」を完成させる。

Step 5　直読直解トレーニング

速読速聴力を高めよう。
（※日本語訳は、英語の原文の順序どおりに記してあります。）

It's that time of year again. Time to go trick-or-treating.
また1年のあの時期です。「トリック・オア・トリート」に出かける時期です。
Make your Halloween a safe one / this year. Remember /
ハロウィーンを安全なものにしましょう、今年は。忘れないように、
to always go trick-or-treating / with an adult /
必ず「トリック・オア・トリート」に行くことを、大人と一緒に、
or a teenaged sibling. Wear a bright costume, or have someone /
または10代のきょうだいと。目立つ服装をして、または誰かに持たせましょう、
in your group carry / a flashlight / so you can be seen / by cars on the road.
グループの、懐中電灯を、あなたが見えるように、路上の車から。
Stick to neighborhoods and houses / you know. Also, remember /
近所と知っている家に限りましょう、知っている。また、覚えておきましょう
fireworks can be dangerous. Light them / only in the presence / of a parent /
花火は危険なことを。それらに点火しましょう、親がいる時だけ、
or other adult. If you just keep / these few safety tips / in mind,
または他の大人が。留めておけば、これらの安全のためのアドバイスを、心に、
you'll have a safe and happy Halloween.
安全で楽しいハロウィーンを過ごせるでしょう。

trick-or-treat：ハロウィーンに菓子をねだって家々をまわる		
sibling：兄弟姉妹	**bright**：派手な	
costume：衣装	**flashlight**：懐中電灯	
stick to：〜に固執する	**neighborhood**：近所	
fireworks：花火	**presence**：存在	
tip：ヒント		

Step 6　基本構文トレーニング

文法・語彙力を高めよう。

61	また、1年のあの時期がやってきました。	It's that time of year again.
62	「トリック・オア・トリート」に出かける時期です。	Time to go trick-or-treating.
63	今年は、ハロウィーンを安全なものにしましょう。	Make your Halloween a safe one this year.
64	必ず大人と一緒に「トリック・オア・トリート」に行くことを忘れないように。	Remember to always go trick-or-treating with an adult.
65	目立つ服装をしてください。	Wear a bright costume.
66	グループの誰かに懐中電灯を持たせましょう。	Have someone in your group carry a flashlight.
67	路上の車からあなたが見えます。	You can be seen by cars on the road.
68	隣近所と知っている家に限りましょう。	Stick to neighborhoods and houses you know.
69	点火をするのは、親がいる時だけにしましょう。	Light them only in the presence of a parent.
70	安全で楽しいハロウィーンを過ごせるでしょう。	You'll have a safe and happy Halloween.

Week 2

Day 3　会話文トレーニング

Step 1　リスニング問題
CD を聞いて、問題を解こう。＜制限時間 2 分＞

Q1. What are the people talking about?
　　(A) Their hobbies
　　(B) Food
　　(C) Work
　　(D) Their families

Q2. At first, how does the man sound?
　　(A) Confident
　　(B) Worried
　　(C) Angry
　　(D) Delighted

Q3. What is the woman's bad news?
　　(A) The team has spent too much money.
　　(B) The project has been cancelled.
　　(C) A team member is very sick.
　　(D) Some changes must be made.

Step 2　リーディング問題

英文を読んで、問題を解こう。＜制限時間3分＞

W: So are you ready for the big day? Everything looks great.
M: No, I still feel we missed something. I mean, this is huge!

W: Just relax. We have a good team behind us. Everything will be fine.
M: If you say so, but I have a sinking feeling something will go wrong.
W: Look, this has been well planned out. You have nothing to worry about.

W: Henry, I have some bad news. I just talked to Sean, and we have some further last-minute requests.
M: I knew it! I told you something was not right.

Q4. Who are the two speakers?
　（A）Designers
　（B）Coworkers
　（C）A married couple
　（D）Managers of a sports group

Q5. How could their attitudes at first be described?
　（A）The woman is not worried but the man is.
　（B）The man is not worried but the woman is.
　（C）Both the man and the woman are worried.
　（D）Neither the man nor the woman is worried.

Q6. At the end of the conversation, whose feeling is confirmed?
　（A）Sean's
　（B）Henry's
　（C）The woman's
　（D）The manager's

Step 3　文法・語彙問題

空欄にふさわしい語句を選ぼう。　＜制限時間2分＞

Q7.　I still feel we _____ something, because there are so many details.
- (A) missed
- (B) miss
- (C) missing
- (D) be missing

Q8.　We have a good team _____ us, so just relax.
- (A) behind
- (B) support
- (C) push
- (D) front of

Q9.　Everything is taken care of, and you have _____ to worry about.
- (A) not
- (B) nothing
- (C) a thing
- (D) anything

Q10.　Everybody's waiting, so are you ready _____ the big day?
- (A) to
- (B) on
- (C) for
- (D) of

Q11.　I have a sinking feeling something will _____ in spite of our work.
- (A) wrong
- (B) get wrong
- (C) go wrong
- (D) go to wrong

Step 4　解答・解説チェック

現時点での理解度を確認しよう。

問題文は、ある重大事項の発表に備える男女の会話です。

1. 正解 **(C)**。質問：「彼らは、何について話していますか？」。答え：「仕事」。ヒント：We have a good team behind us., this has been well planned out.
2. 正解 **(B)**。質問：「会話の最初で、男性の口調はどうですか？」。答え：「心配している」。ヒント：I still feel we missed something.
3. 正解 **(D)**。質問：「女性の悪い知らせは、何ですか？」。答え：「少し変更が必要である」。ヒント：we have some further last-minute requests.
4. 正解 **(B)**。質問：「話し手は、どんな人たちですか？」。答え：「同僚」。ヒント：Q1同様。
5. 正解 **(A)**。質問：「当初、2人の態度はどのように描写されていましたか？」。答え：「女性は不安を感じていなかったが、男性は感じていた」。ヒント：女性のEverything looks great. と、男性のI still feel we missed something.
6. 正解 **(B)**。質問：「会話の終わりに、誰の気持ちが確かなものになりましたか？」。答え：「ヘンリーの」。ヒント：I told you something was not right.
7. 正解 **(A)**。過去に見落としたことが気になっているので、過去形 missed を選ぶ。
8. 正解 **(A)**。文意から、have ～ behind +（人）「（人）を支える～がいる」を完成させる。
9. 正解 **(B)**。文意から、have nothing to + 動詞「～するものは何もない」を完成させる。
10. 正解 **(C)**。be ready for「～の準備ができている」の疑問文を完成させる。
11. 正解 **(C)**。文意から、go wrong「うまくいかない」を選ぶ。

Step 5　直読直解トレーニング

速読速聴力を高めよう。

(※日本語訳は、英語の原文の順序どおりに記してあります。)

W: So / are you ready / for the big day?
さて、準備できていますか、大事な日の？
Everything looks great.
すべてうまくいっているようですね。

M: No, I still feel / we missed something. I mean, this is huge!
いや、まだ気がします、何か見落としている。つまり、大がかりだから！

W: Just relax. We have a good team / behind us.
落ち着いて。すばらしいチームがいます、われわれを支えてくれる。
Everything will be fine.
すべてうまくいくでしょう。

M: If you say so, but I have a sinking feeling / something will go wrong.
そう言うのなら、でも不安感があります、何かがうまくいかない。

W: Look, this has been well planned out.
いいですか、これは十分に計画されてきました。
You have nothing / to worry about.
何もありません、心配することは。

W: Henry, I have some bad news.
ヘンリー、悪い知らせがあります。
I just talked to Sean, and we have / some further last-minute requests.
ショーンと話したところです、あります、土壇場での追加のお願いが。

M: I knew it! I told you / something was not right.
そうだと思っていました！　言いましたよね、何かおかしいって。

語句

the big day：大事な日　**miss**：〜を見落とす　**I mean,**：つまり　**huge**：巨大な
sinking feeling：不安感　**go wrong**：うまくいかない　**plan out**：十分に計画する
further：さらなる　**last-minute**：土壇場の　**request**：依頼

Step 6　基本構文トレーニング

文法・語彙力を高めよう。

71	大事な日の準備はできていますか？	Are you ready for the big day?
72	すべて、うまくいっているようです。	Everything looks great.
73	まだ、何か忘れている気がします。	I still feel we missed something.
74	われわれを支えてくれるすばらしいチームがいます。	We have a good team behind us.
75	きっと、すべてうまくいきます。	Everything will be fine.
76	何かがうまくいかない不安感があります。	I have a sinking feeling something will go wrong.
77	これは、十分に計画されてきました。	This has been well planned out.
78	心配することは、何もありません。	You have nothing to worry about.
79	そうだと思っていました！	I knew it!
80	何かがおかしいって言いましたよね。	I told you something was not right.

Day 4　説明文トレーニング

Step 1　リスニング問題
CDを聞いて、問題を解こう。＜制限時間2分＞

Q1. When was the announcement probably made?
　　(A) At the start of spring
　　(B) In the middle of winter
　　(C) Just before autumn
　　(D) In early spring

Q2. Who will find the passage most useful?
　　(A) Homeowners
　　(B) Residences of high-rise apartment buildings
　　(C) Students living in dorms
　　(D) Teenagers looking for part-time jobs

Q3. What does a person have to do to use the Vac 3000?
　　(A) Use it like a leaf blower
　　(B) Just hold the tool
　　(C) Mulch the leaves after the bag is empty
　　(D) Bend and twist to get to leaves

Step 2　リーディング問題
英文を読んで、問題を解こう。＜制限時間 3 分＞

Fall is a time for the leaves to change color. Fall can be beautiful in all its splendor. But when those leaves fall, whose job is it to rake them up? Raking leaves can be backbreaking work. Even using a leaf blower can be a pain. What's the solution? The Autumn Vac 3000. With its patented vibra-suction action, the Autumn Vac 3000 sucks up all those nasty wet leaves and it even mulches them before you empty the bag. Plus the extender hose means no more bending and twisting to get at those leaves. The Autumn Vac 3000— get it at stores everywhere!

Q4.　What is this passage mainly about?
　　（A）A leaf blower
　　（B）The price of the Autumn Vac
　　（C）The beauty of leaves in the fall
　　（D）A piece of equipment that saves labor

Q5.　What is said about the extender hose?
　　（A）It uses a special, patented action.
　　（B）It is available for a small extra cost.
　　（C）It can be ordered from the manufacturer.
　　（D）It makes backbreaking work unnecessary.

Q6.　How many actions of the Autumn Vac are mentioned?
　　（A）One
　　（B）Two
　　（C）Three
　　（D）Four

Step 3　文法・語彙問題
空欄にふさわしい語句を選ぼう。　＜制限時間2分＞

Q7. Fall is a time for the leaves _____ color as the weather turns cooler.
   (A) change
   (B) changed
   (C) to change
   (D) are changed

Q8. Fall can be beautiful in _____ its splendor of leaves changing colors.
   (A) all
   (B) anything
   (C) total
   (D) most

Q9. What's the _____ to that problem?
   (A) solve
   (B) solid
   (C) solving
   (D) solution

Q10. It sucks up all those nasty wet _____ that usually are hard to pick up.
   (A) leaf
   (B) leave
   (C) leaves
   (D) leaving

Q11. The extender hose means no more _____ to pick up the leaves.
   (A) to bend
   (B) bent
   (C) being bent
   (D) bending

Step 4　解答・解説チェック

現時点での理解度を確認しよう。

問題文は、落ち葉掃除を楽にする掃除機の広告文です。

1. 正解 **(C)**。質問：「この案内は、いつ行なわれたと思われますか？」。答え：「秋になる少し前」。ヒント：Fall is a time for the leaves to change color.
2. 正解 **(A)**。質問：「この文書が、もっとも役に立つのは誰ですか？」。答え：「家の所有者」。ヒント：Raking leaves can be backbreaking work.
3. 正解 **(B)**。質問：「バック3000を使うために、しなければならないことは何ですか？」。答え：「器具を手に持つことだけ」。ヒント：後半の文から。
4. 正解 **(D)**。質問：「この文書は、主に何についてですか？」。答え：「肉体労働を省くための器具」。ヒント：What's the solution? The Autumn Vac 3000.
5. 正解 **(D)**。質問：「延長ホースについて、どんなことが言われていますか？」。答え：「骨の折れる作業が不要になる」。ヒント：the extender hose means no more bending and twisting
6. 正解 **(B)**。質問：「オータム・バックの動作が、いくつ述べられていますか？」。答え：「2つ」。ヒント：sucks up all those nasty wet leaves, it even mulches
7. 正解 **(C)**。to change を選び、time for +（人・物）+ to + 動詞「（人・物）が〜する時」を完成させる。
8. 正解 **(A)**。強調の副詞 all を選び、in all its splendor「（それの）見事さが最盛期である」を完成させる。
9. 正解 **(D)**。文意から、名詞 solution「解決策」を選ぶ。(A)「〜を解決する」（動詞）、(B)「堅い」（形容詞）、(C)「解決すること」（動名詞）。
10. 正解 **(C)**。those のあとなので、名詞は複数形。leaves（複数形）を選ぶ。
11. 正解 **(D)**。no more のあとには、名詞（相当語句）がくるので、bending「かがむこと」（動名詞）を選ぶ。

Step 5　直読直解トレーニング

速読速聴力を高めよう。

（※日本語訳は、英語の原文の順序どおりに記してあります。）

Fall is a time / for the leaves to change color. Fall can be beautiful /
秋は季節です、紅葉の。秋は、美しいかもしれません、
in all its splendor. But when those leaves fall, whose job is it /
その見事さで。しかしそれらの葉が散った時、誰の仕事なのでしょう
to rake them up? Raking leaves / can be backbreaking work.
それらをかき集めるのは？　落ち葉をかき集めるのは、重労働です。
Even using a leaf blower / can be a pain. What's the solution?
リーフ・ブロワーを使っても、苦痛です。解決策は何でしょう？
The Autumn Vac 3000. With its patented vibra-suction action,
オータム・バック3000です。特許振動吸い取り動作で、
the Autumn Vac 3000 / sucks up all those nasty wet leaves /
オータム・バック3000は汚い湿った落ち葉を全部吸い上げます、
and it even mulches them / before you empty the bag. Plus /
さらにそれらを腐葉土にさえします、袋を空にする前に。しかも、
the extender hose means / no more bending and twisting /
延長ホースは意味します、もうかがんだり身をよじったりが不要で、
to get at those leaves. The Autumn Vac 3000 — get it at stores everywhere!
落ち葉に届くことを。オータム・バック3000、全国のお店でお求めください。

語句

splendor：見事さ	**rake**：〜をかき集める
backbreaking：骨の折れる	**patented**：特許取得済みの
suck：〜を吸い込む	**nasty**：汚らしい
mulch：〜を腐葉土にする	**empty**：〜を空にする
bend：かがむ	**twist**：身をよじる

Step 6　基本構文トレーニング

文法・語彙力を高めよう。

81	秋は紅葉の季節です。	Fall is a time for the leaves to change color.
82	秋は、その見事さで美しいかもしれません。	Fall can be beautiful in all its splendor.
83	それらをかき集めるのは誰の仕事なのでしょう？	Whose job is it to rake them up?
84	落ち葉をかき集めるのは重労働です。	Raking leaves can be backbreaking work.
85	リーフ・ブロワーを使っても苦痛です。	Even using a leaf blower can be a pain.
86	解決策は、何でしょう？	What's the solution?
87	それは、汚い湿った落ち葉を全部吸い上げます。	It sucks up all those nasty wet leaves.
88	袋を空にする前に、それらを腐葉土にさえします。	It even mulches them before you empty the bag.
89	延長ホースで、もうかがむのは不要です。	The extender hose means no more bending.
90	全国のお店でお求めください。	Get it at stores everywhere.

Day 5　会話文トレーニング

Step 1　リスニング問題
CDを聞いて、問題を解こう。＜制限時間2分＞

Q1. What was the tone of the conversation?

　(A) Hateful
　(B) Serious
　(C) Friendly
　(D) Mysterious

Q2. Where did the conversation take place?

　(A) In the man's home
　(B) In the woman's home
　(C) In a restaurant
　(D) In Alaska

Q3. What are the man and Marla planning to do?

　(A) Get married
　(B) Visit Alaska
　(C) Have an adventure
　(D) Visit Grandma Bragg as often as they can

Step 2　リーディング問題

英文を読んで、問題を解こう。＜制限時間 3 分＞

W: So you're my Marla's fiancé. My, what a strapping young man you are!
M: So, Grandma Bragg, I hear you really like traveling. Where did you go last?

W: Well, that's my latest adventure. As I said, Alaska was amazing, even for an old woman like me.
M: You're not old! I'll bet you're not a day over 65.
W: Oh, you flatter me, young man. Want to know a secret? I'm 77!

W: Well, Jack, you are welcome here anytime at all.
M: I'm glad we've had this chance to get to know each other a little better.

Q4. Who is Marla?
   (A) Jack's wife
   (B) Jack's grandmother
   (C) Mrs. Bragg's daughter
   (D) The woman Jack plans to marry

Q5. How old does Jack say he thinks Mrs. Bragg is?
   (A) Less than 65   (B) No more than 65
   (C) Between 65 and 77   (D) No more than 77

Q6. What was Mrs. Bragg's opinion of Jack when the visit ended?
   (A) She liked him.
   (B) She had not decided.
   (C) She did not want to see him again.
   (D) She thought he was too young to get married.

Step 3　文法・語彙問題

空欄にふさわしい語句を選ぼう。　＜制限時間2分＞

Q7. That's my _____ adventure, and I'm planning another one.
- (A) last one
- (B) latest
- (C) the latest
- (D) lately

Q8. You're not old; I'll bet _____ not a day over 65.
- (A) you're
- (B) you'll
- (C) you'd
- (D) you've

Q9. I'm glad we've had this _____ to know each other better.
- (A) check
- (B) chance
- (C) charge
- (D) change

Q10. I hear you really _____ traveling, but is that true?
- (A) liking
- (B) like to
- (C) like
- (D) are liking

Q11. You are welcome here _____ at all, so please visit again.
- (A) anything
- (B) anytime
- (C) anywhere
- (D) anyway

Step 4　解答・解説チェック

現時点での理解度を確認しよう。

問題文は、老婦人とその孫のフィアンセとの会話です。

1. 正解 **(C)**。質問：「会話の雰囲気は、どうでしたか？」。答え：「友好的」。ヒント：会話全体の内容から。
2. 正解 **(B)**。質問：「この会話は、どこで行なわれましたか？」。答え：「女性の家」。ヒント：女性の Well, Jack, you are welcome here anytime at all.
3. 正解 **(A)**。質問：「男性とマーラは、何をする予定ですか？」。答え：「結婚」。ヒント：女性の So you're my Marla's fiancé.
4. 正解 **(D)**。質問：「マーラは誰ですか？」。答え：「ジャックが結婚を予定している女性」。ヒント：So you're my Marla's fiancé.
5. 正解 **(B)**。質問：「ジャックは、ブラッグ夫人を何歳だと思ったと言っていますか？」。答え：「65歳以下」。ヒント：I'll bet you're not a day over 65. (A) は「65歳未満」で不可。
6. 正解 **(A)**。質問：「訪問を終えた時のブラッグ夫人のジャックについての意見はどうですか？」。答え：「気に入った」。ヒント：I'm glad we've had this chance to get to know each other
7. 正解 **(B)**。名詞 adventure「冒険」を修飾するので、形容詞 latest「いちばん最近の」を選ぶ。my（所有格代名詞）があるので、(C) は不可。
8. 正解 **(A)**。「あなたは65歳を1日たりとも超えていない」という文意から、you're を選ぶ。
9. 正解 **(B)**。選択肢はすべて名詞。文意から、chance「機会」を選ぶ。(A)「照合」、(C)「料金」、(D)「変化」。
10. 正解 **(C)**。like を選び、like + 動詞 ing「～するのが好き」を完成させる。
11. 正解 **(B)**。anytime を選び、at all「いつでも」の強調形を完成させる。

Week 2

Step 5　直読直解トレーニング
速読速聴力を高めよう。

(※日本語訳は、英語の原文の順序どおりに記してあります。)

W: So you're my Marla's fiancé. My, what a strapping young man you are!
では、あなたがマーラの婚約者ね。まあ、なんていい体格の若者なの！

M: So, Grandma Bragg, I hear / you really like traveling.
あのう、ブラッグさん、聞いています、あなたは旅行がとても好きだと。
Where did you go last?
最後に行ったのはどこですか？

W: Well, that's my latest adventure. As I said,
まあ、それが私のいちばん最近の冒険です。言ったように、
Alaska was amazing, even for an old woman / like me.
アラスカはすばらしかったです、年取った女性にも、私のような。

M: You're not old! I'll bet / you're not a day over 65.
年寄りじゃありません！　確信します、65歳を1日も超えていないと。

W: Oh, you flatter me, young man. Want to know a secret? I'm 77!
まあ、お世辞がおじょうずね、あなた。秘密を知りたい？　私77歳よ！

W: Well, Jack, you are welcome here / anytime at all.
さて、ジャック、あなたここでは大歓迎です、いつでも。

M: I'm glad / we've had this chance / to get to know each other /
嬉しいです、この機会が持てて、おたがいを知るための、
a little better.
もっとよく。

語句	
fiancé：婚約者	**strapping**：背の高くてがっしりした
grandma：おばあちゃん	**last**：最後に
latest：いちばん最近の	**adventure**：冒険
amazing：見事な	**bet**：〜と確信する
flatter：〜にお世辞を言う	**welcome**：〜を歓迎する

Step 6　基本構文トレーニング

文法・語彙力を高めよう。

91	なんていい体格の若者なのでしょう、あなたって！	What a strapping young man you are!
92	あなたは旅行がとても好きだと聞いています。	I hear you really like traveling.
93	最後に行ったのはどこですか？	Where did you go last?
94	それが私のいちばん最近の冒険です。	That's my latest adventure.
95	言ったように、アラスカはすばらしかったです。	As I said, Alaska was amazing.
96	65歳を1日たりとも超えていないはずです。	I'll bet you're not a day over 65.
97	まあ、お世辞がじょうずですね。	Oh, you flatter me.
98	秘密を知りたいですか？	Want to know a secret?
99	あなたは、ここではいつでも大歓迎です。	You are welcome here anytime at all.
100	この機会が持てて嬉しいです。	I'm glad we've had this chance.

Day 6 チェックテスト

ふさわしい語句の意味を選ぼう。　＜制限時間5分＞

1. be into：(A) 〜の中に入る　(B) 〜に夢中　(C) 〜に存在する
2. favorite：(A) 香りのよい　(B) 熱のある　(C) お気に入りの
3. on tour：(A) ツアー中　(B) 一時停止中　(C) 再生中
4. rephrase：(A) 〜を言い換える　(B) とめどなく話す　(C) 繰り返す
5. decade：(A) 過去　(B) 1世紀　(C) 10年間
6. burn：(A) 〜を焼く　(B) 〜を埋める　(C) 忙しい
7. update：(A) 〜を更新する　(B) 日付を繰り上げる　(C) 最近の
8. musical：(A) 楽器　(B) 音声　(C) 音楽の
9. taste：(A) 嗜好　(B) 噛む　(C) テスト
10. cool：(A) つまらない　(B) すばらしい　(C) おもしろい

11. trick-or-treat：(A) ハロウィーンに菓子をねだって家々をまわる
    　　　　　　　　(B) サーカス　(C) 大道芸
12. sibling：(A) 寒い　(B) 親戚　(C) 兄弟姉妹
13. bright：(A) 派手な　(B) 持ってくる　(C) 正しい
14. costume：(A) 道具　(B) 食器　(C) 衣装
15. flashlight：(A) 懐中電灯　(B) 灯光器　(C) 蛍光灯
16. stick to：(A) 棒を立てる　(B) 積み重ねる　(C) 〜に固執する
17. neighborhood：(A) 市街　(B) 近所　(C) 隣町
18. fireworks：(A) 消防署　(B) 花火　(C) 火事
19. presence：(A) 贈り物　(B) 存在　(C) 現在の
20. tip：(A) ヒント　(B) アイデア　(C) コンセプト

21. the big day：(A) 給料日　(B) 大事な日　(C) 元日
22. miss：(A) 〜を見落とす　(B) 〜を見つける　(C) 〜を見る
23. I mean,：(A) つまり　(B) 一般的に　(C) それどころか
24. huge：(A) 空腹の　(B) 抱きしめる　(C) 巨大な

25. sinking feeling：(A) よく考える　(B) 不安感　(C) 論理的思考
26. go wrong：(A) 方向違い　(B) 長距離を行く　(C) うまくいかない
27. plan out：(A) 計画を中止する　(B) 十分に計画する
　　　　　　(C) 計画を破棄する
28. further：(A) さらなる　(B) 羽　(C) より遠くの
29. last-minute：(A) 土壇場の　(B) 最後の　(C) ついさっきの
30. request：(A) 拒否　(B) 操作　(C) 依頼

31. splendor：(A) スマートな　(B) 見事さ　(C) 輝き
32. rake：(A) 〜を漏らす　(B) 湖　(C) 〜をかき集める
33. backbreaking：(A) 骨の折れる　(B) 躍進　(C) 打ち解ける
34. patented：(A) のり付けの　(B) 特許取得済みの　(C) 付き添いの
35. suck：(A) 〜を止める　(B) 〜を吸い込む　(C) 〜を吐き出す
36. nasty：(A) 汚らしい　(B) 長続きする　(C) 豊かな
37. mulch：(A) 〜を増やす　(B) たくさんの　(C) 〜を腐葉土にする
38. empty：(A) 〜を空にする　(B) 〜に力を与える　(C) 〜を誘惑する
39. bend：(A) 寄りかかる　(B) お辞儀をする　(C) かがむ
40. twist：(A) 伏せる　(B) 飛び跳ねる　(C) 身をよじる

41. fiancé：(A) フランス人　(B) 投資家　(C) 婚約者
42. strapping：(A) 活動的な　(B) きゃしゃな
　　　　　　　(C) 背の高くてがっしりした
43. grandma：(A) おばあちゃん　(B) おじいちゃん
　　　　　　 (C) ひいおばあちゃん
44. last：(A) 最初に　(B) 最後に　(C) 中間に
45. latest：(A) いちばん昔の　(B) いちばん古い　(C) いちばん最近の
46. adventure：(A) 苦行　(B) 冒険　(C) 安泰
47. amazing：(A) 失敗した　(B) 見事な　(C) 困惑した
48. bet：(A) 〜と確信する　(B) 寝床　(C) よりよい
49. flatter：(A) 〜にお世辞を言う　(B) 〜に愚痴を言う
　　　　　　(C) 〜を非難する
50. welcome：(A) 〜に行く　(B) 〜を歓迎する　(C) 〜に伝える

チェックテスト解答

1. **(B)**	2. **(C)**	3. **(A)**	4. **(A)**	5. **(C)**
6. **(A)**	7. **(A)**	8. **(C)**	9. **(A)**	10. **(B)**
11. **(A)**	12. **(C)**	13. **(A)**	14. **(C)**	15. **(A)**
16. **(C)**	17. **(B)**	18. **(B)**	19. **(B)**	20. **(A)**
21. **(B)**	22. **(A)**	23. **(A)**	24. **(C)**	25. **(B)**
26. **(C)**	27. **(B)**	28. **(A)**	29. **(A)**	30. **(C)**
31. **(B)**	32. **(C)**	33. **(A)**	34. **(B)**	35. **(B)**
36. **(A)**	37. **(C)**	38. **(A)**	39. **(C)**	40. **(C)**
41. **(C)**	42. **(C)**	43. **(A)**	44. **(B)**	45. **(C)**
46. **(B)**	47. **(B)**	48. **(A)**	49. **(A)**	50. **(B)**

<ワンポイント>

　第2週のトレーニングはいかがでしたか？　設問（Q1～Q6）を素早く理解できるようになってきましたか？　設問が素早く理解できるようになってきたら、問題形式に慣れてきたと考えていいと思います。

　しかし、問題形式には慣れてきたけれど、「英語がさっぱり聞き取れない」という方も多いはずです。リスニング上達のコツは、いきなり母国語のように100％聞き取れることを期待しないこと。70％聞き取れたら十分ぐらいの気持ちで「リラックスして聞く」ことです。

　わからないところがあっても、気にしない。わからないところに意識を向けるのではなく、わかったところから想像する。いい力の加減で聞きましょう。リスニング力は、想像力。会話やスピーチの場面（WhoとWhere）を想像しながら聞いて、問題を解きながら、わからなかったところも想像してみましょう。

第 4 章

Week 3

Week 3
今週のトレーニング

	Day 1〜 Day 5 のトレーニング	
Step	内容	時間
1	リスニング問題（3問）	2分
2	リーディング問題（3問）	3分
3	文法・語彙問題（5問）	2分
4	解答・解説チェック	3分
5	直読直解トレーニング ① CD（英語）を聞いて、英文を目で追う。 ② CD（英語）を聞いて、日本語訳を目で追う。 ③ カンマ (,)、ピリオド (.)、スラッシュ (/) の単位で、英文の意味が理解できるか確認（理解できない部分は、日本語訳や語彙を参照）。	5〜15分
6	基本構文トレーニング ① 1文ずつCD（日本語・英語）を聞き、英語を数回音読。 ② 10文の英語を続けて音読（数回行なう）。 ③ テキストを縦に半分に折るなどして日本語訳を隠し、英語部分を見て意味がすぐにわかるか確認。 ④ 応用トレーニング「ルックアップ＆セイ」「音読筆写」	5〜15分

＜ワンポイント＞

　先週の応用トレーニング「ルックアップ＆セイ」（50ページ）を、試してみましたか？　どうしても顔を上げて言えない基本構文は、音読筆写をしてみると、しっかり覚えることができます。

音読筆写	英文を声に出しながら、スピードを上げて5回書き写します（字は乱れてOK）。終了したら、顔を上げ、英語を話します（言えなかったらあと2回音読筆写）。

Day 1 会話文トレーニング

Step 1 リスニング問題
CD を聞いて、問題を解こう。＜制限時間 2 分＞

Q1. What are the two people doing?
    (A) Working
    (B) Running
    (C) Sweating
    (D) Cheating

Q2. At first, how is the weather?
    (A) Hot and humid
    (B) Rainy
    (C) Windy
    (D) Fine

Q3. Why did the woman go to the coffee shop?
    (A) It suddenly got very hot.
    (B) She needed a cool drink.
    (C) It was starting to rain.
    (D) She wanted to use the restroom.

Step 2　リーディング問題

英文を読んで、問題を解こう。＜制限時間３分＞

M: What a glorious day! So what route shall we take today?
W: Let's head toward the park and do the full circuit today. I really need to build up a good sweat.

M: Those clouds look ominous. Maybe we should pick up the pace a little.
W: If it comes, it's only rain. It'll help cool us off.
M: Last time you said that, we got caught in a thunderstorm.

M: Here it comes. I'm running for cover. Race you to that coffee shop over there.
W: Hey, that's cheating. You never said "Go!"

Q4. How is the weather from the beginning to the end of this dialogue?
　　(A) It remains bad.
　　(B) It remains good.
　　(C) It changes from bad to good.
　　(D) It changes from good to bad.

Q5. How do the speakers feel about the weather?
　　(A) The woman is worried about it but the man is not.
　　(B) The man is worried about it but the woman is not.
　　(C) Both are worried about it.
　　(D) Neither is worried about it.

Q6. Why are they going to a coffee shop?
　　(A) For some coffee　　　　(B) For protection against the weather
　　(C) Because they are cold　　(D) Because they are tired

Step 3　文法・語彙問題

空欄にふさわしい語句を選ぼう。　＜制限時間2分＞

Q7. Let's _____ toward the park and do the full circuit.
　　(A) set
　　(B) direct
　　(C) head
　　(D) foot

Q8. I really need to build _____ a good sweat.
　　(A) out
　　(B) up
　　(C) on
　　(D) down

Q9. I think it's going to rain, because those _____ look ominous.
　　(A) clouds
　　(B) clowns
　　(C) crowds
　　(D) crows

Q10. Maybe we should _____ up the pace a little.
　　(A) put
　　(B) go
　　(C) pick
　　(D) get

Q11. We _____ in a thunderstorm the last time we went there.
　　(A) caught
　　(B) had caught
　　(C) had to catch
　　(D) got caught

Step 4　解答・解説チェック

現時点での理解度を確認しよう。

問題文は、ジョギングをする男女の変わりつつある天候についての会話です。

1. 正解 **(B)**。質問：「2人は、何をしていますか？」。答え：「ランニング」。ヒント：So what route, Let's head toward the park, Maybe we should pick up the pace a little.
2. 正解 **(D)**。質問：「最初のうち、天気はどうですか？」。答え：「晴れ」。ヒント：What a glorious day!
3. 正解 **(C)**。質問：「女性は、なぜコーヒーショップに行きましたか？」。答え：「雨が降り出した」。ヒント：Here it comes. I'm running for cover.
4. 正解 **(D)**。質問：「会話の始めから終わりまでの天気は、どうですか？」。答え：「好天から悪天候に変わる」。ヒント：What a glorious day!, Those clouds look ominous., Here it comes.
5. 正解 **(B)**。質問：「話し手たちの天気に対する気持ちは、どうですか？」。答え：「男性は心配しているが、女性は気にしていない」。ヒント：男性の Maybe we should pick up the pace a little, 女性の It'll help cool us off.
6. 正解 **(B)**。質問：「彼らは、なぜコーヒーショップに行くのですか？」。答え：「悪天候を避けるため」。ヒント：I'm running for cover.
7. 正解 **(C)**。head toward「〜へ向かう」を完成させる。
8. 正解 **(B)**。build up a good sweat「たっぷり汗をかく」を完成させる。
9. 正解 **(A)**。選択肢はすべて名詞の複数形。文意から、clouds「雲」を選ぶ。(B)「道化師」、(C)「群衆」、(D)「カラス」。
10. 正解 **(C)**。文意から、pick up the pace「ペースを上げる」を完成させる。
11. 正解 **(D)**。文意から、get caught in「(ありがたくないこと) に遭遇する」の過去形を完成させる。

Step 5　直読直解トレーニング

速読速聴力を高めよう。

（※日本語訳は、英語の原文の順序どおりに記してあります。）

M:　What a glorious day! So / what route shall we take today?
　　なんてすばらしい天気！　では、今日はどのコースにしましょうか？

W:　Let's head toward the park / and do the full circuit today.
　　公園のほうへ行きましょう、そして、今日は完全に一周しましょう。
　　I really need to build up / a good sweat.
　　かかなければなりません、たっぷり汗を。

M:　Those clouds look ominous.
　　雲行きが怪しいです。
　　Maybe we should pick up the pace / a little.
　　ペースを上げたほうがいいかもしれません、少し。

W:　If it comes, it's only rain. It'll help cool us off.
　　降ったとしても、たかが雨ですよ。われわれを涼しくしてくれます。

M:　Last time you said that, we got caught in a thunderstorm.
　　この前あなたがそう言った時、われわれは雷雨にあいました。

M:　Here it comes. I'm running for cover.
　　降ってきました。急いで雨宿りです。
　　Race you to that coffee shop / over there.
　　あのコーヒーショップまで競走しましょう、あそこの。

W:　Hey, that's cheating. You never said "Go!"
　　ねえ、それはずるいです。あなたは「スタート」と言っていません。

語句

- **glorious**：好天の
- **circuit**：1周
- **ominous**：不気味な
- **cool off**：〜を涼しくする
- **cover**：避難場所
- **head toward**：〜に向かう
- **good sweat**：たっぷりの汗
- **pick up the pace**：ペースを上げる
- **thunderstorm**：雷雨
- **cheat**：いかさまをする

Step 6　基本構文トレーニング

文法・語彙力を高めよう。

101	なんてすばらしい天気でしょう！	What a glorious day!
102	今日はどのコースにしましょうか？	What route shall we take today?
103	公園のほうへ行きましょう。	Let's head toward the park.
104	たっぷり汗をかかなければなりません。	I really need to build up a good sweat.
105	雲行きが怪しいです。	Those clouds look ominous.
106	われわれは、少しペースを上げたほうがいいかもしれません。	Maybe we should pick up the pace a little.
107	降ったとしても、たかが雨です。	If it comes, it's only rain.
108	われわれは、雷雨にあいました。	We got caught in a thunderstorm.
109	あそこのコーヒーショップまで競走しましょう。	Race you to that coffee shop over there.
110	あなたは、「スタート」と言っていません。	You never said "Go!"

Day 2 説明文トレーニング

Step 1 リスニング問題
CDを聞いて、問題を解こう。＜制限時間2分＞

Q1. Which in Paris is discussed in the talk?
   (A) Its restaurants
   (B) Its churches
   (C) Its shops
   (D) Its monuments

Q2. How many prices are shown on goods at sale times?
   (A) One
   (B) Two
   (C) Three
   (D) Four

Q3. According to this advice, when should someone go to Paris?
   (A) In January or July
   (B) In January or February
   (C) In July or August
   (D) In August or December

Step 2　リーディング問題

英文を読んで、問題を解こう。＜制限時間３分＞

Paris is one of the most expensive cities for shopping in the world. It doesn't have to be that way, however. Just time your vacation right, and do what Parisians do. Twice a year they do their serious shopping for brand names like Gucci, Hermès, Valentino, and Chanel. In the months of July and January, Parisians go shopping mad, so be prepared to battle it out. Stores slash prices even more drastically as those months draw to a close. Plus, the law requires shops to show the original retail price of each sale item. This lets you see how much you're actually saving.

Q4. Who is this advice intended for?
　　(A) Rich people
　　(B) Visitors to Paris
　　(C) People living in Paris
　　(D) Americans and Canadians

Q5. According to the passage, when are the best bargains available?
　　(A) At the end of January
　　(B) Anytime in January
　　(C) At the beginning of July
　　(D) Anytime except January and July

Q6. What warning is given readers?
　　(A) Some sale items are not really bargains.
　　(B) Stores can be dangerous places during sales.
　　(C) There is not a large supply of brand-name products.
　　(D) They will have to compete with Parisians.

Step 3　文法・語彙問題

空欄にふさわしい語句を選ぼう。　＜制限時間2分＞

Q7. Paris is one of _____ expensive cities for shopping in the world.
   (A) most
   (B) the most
   (C) almost
   (D) at most

Q8. Twice a year they do their _____ shopping for brand names.
   (A) seriously
   (B) seriousness
   (C) serious
   (D) series

Q9. If you are thinking of going shopping then, be prepared to battle it _____.
   (A) up
   (B) away
   (C) out
   (D) in

Q10. The law _____ shops to show the original price of each sale item.
   (A) require
   (B) requires
   (C) requiring
   (D) is required

Q11. This lets you _____ how much you're saving by getting those bargains.
   (A) see
   (B) to see
   (C) seeing
   (D) to seeing

Step 4　解答・解説チェック

現時点での理解度を確認しよう。

問題文は、物価の高いパリでの上手な買い物のヒントを述べたものです。

1. 正解 **(C)**。質問：「話では、パリの何について述べていますか？」。答え：「お店」。ヒント：Paris is ... for shopping
2. 正解 **(B)**。質問：「セールの時期には、商品にいくつ値段が表示されますか？」。答え：「2つ」。ヒント：the law requires shops to show the original retail price of each sale item.
3. 正解 **(A)**。質問：「このアドバイスによれば、パリにはいつ行くべきですか？」。答え：「1月か7月」。ヒント：In the months of July and January, Parisians go shopping mad
4. 正解 **(B)**。質問：「このアドバイスは、誰に向けられたものですか？」。答え：「パリを訪れる人びと」。ヒント：Just time your vacation right, and do what Parisians do.
5. 正解 **(A)**。質問：「この文書によると、いちばんよいバーゲンは、いつですか？」。答え：「1月末」。ヒント：In the months of July and January, Stores slash prices even more drastically as those months draw to a close.
6. 正解 **(D)**。質問：「読み手に対し、どんな注意が与えられていますか？」。答え：「パリの住民と競わなければならない」。ヒント：Parisians go shopping mad, so be prepared to battle it out.
7. 正解 **(B)**。one of + 形容詞（最上級）で、「もっとも～の1つ」。the most expensive を完成させる。
8. 正解 **(C)**。shopping（動名詞）を修飾する形容詞 serious を選び、serious shopping「本格的なまとめ買い」を完成させる。
9. 正解 **(C)**。文意から、battle it out「死闘を演じる」を完成させる。
10. 正解 **(B)**。文意から、require +（人）+ to + 動詞「（人）に～するよう命じる」を完成させる。The law（主語）が単数なので、requires（三人称単数形）を選ぶ。
11. 正解 **(A)**。see を選び、let +（人）+ 動詞「（人）に～させる」を完成させる。

Step 5　直読直解トレーニング
速読速聴力を高めよう。
（※日本語訳は、英語の原文の順序どおりに記してあります。）

Paris is one of the most expensive cities / for shopping / in the world.
パリはもっとも高い都市の１つです、物価の、世界で。
It doesn't have to be that way, however. Just time your vacation right,
必ずしもそうとは限りません、しかし。休暇の時期をうまく選び、
and do what Parisians do. Twice a year / they do their serious shopping /
パリ市民がするようにしてください。年２回、彼らは本気で買い物します、
for brand names / like Gucci, Hermès, Valentino, and Chanel.
ブランド品の、グッチ、エルメス、バレンチノ、シャネルなどの。
In the months of July and January, Parisians go shopping mad,
７月と１月に、パリ市民は夢中で買い物をします、
so be prepared to battle it out. Stores slash prices / even more drastically /
ですから死闘を覚悟してください。店は値下げをします、さらに思い切った、
as those months draw to a close. Plus, the law requires shops /
これらの月が月末に近づくと。しかも、法律は店に要求しています、
to show the original retail price / of each sale item. This lets you see /
もとの小売価格を表示することを、どのセール対象品にも。これでわかります、
how much you're actually saving.
実際にいくら節約できているのかが。

語句

- **time**：〜の時期を選ぶ
- **brand name**：ブランド品
- **battle it out**：徹底的に戦う
- **drastically**：大幅に
- **retail**：小売りの
- **serious**：本気の
- **be prepared**：備える
- **slash**：（価格を）下げる
- **draw to a close**：終わりに近づく
- **item**：商品

Step 6　基本構文トレーニング

文法・語彙力を高めよう。

CD 48

111	パリはもっとも物価の高い都市の1つです。	Paris is one of the most expensive cities for shopping.
112	必ずしもそうであるとは限りません。	It doesn't have to be that way.
113	休暇の時期をうまく選んでください。	Just time your vacation right.
114	パリ市民のするようにしてください。	Do what Parisians do.
115	年2回、彼らは本気で買い物をします。	Twice a year they do their serious shopping.
116	パリ市民は、夢中で買い物をします。	Parisians go shopping mad.
117	死闘を覚悟してください。	Be prepared to battle it out.
118	店は、さらに思い切った値下げをします。	Stores slash prices even more drastically.
119	法律は、店にもとの値段を表示するよう要求しています。	The law requires shops to show the original price.
120	これで、いくら節約できているのかがわかります。	This lets you see how much you're saving.

Day 3 会話文トレーニング

Step 1 リスニング問題
CDを聞いて、問題を解こう。＜制限時間2分＞

Q1. Where are the people?
   (A) In line at a restaurant
   (B) At work
   (C) At home
   (D) In a parking lot

Q2. What is the man going to do at lunchtime?
   (A) Ask for suggestions
   (B) Give out some information
   (C) Buy sandwiches for everyone
   (D) Go home early

Q3. How were exports last year?
   (A) Better than now
   (B) Worse than now
   (C) Almost the same as now
   (D) Exactly the same as now

Step 2　リーディング問題

英文を読んで、問題を解こう。＜制限時間 3 分＞

W: Nick, can I have a word with you? The line is really slow today.
M: I was going to inform everyone at lunchtime. We've had to slow down production.

W: So, any idea when things will be back up to speed?
M: In a few weeks. Just hang in there. Demand is down just a bit right now.
W: Is there any reason why? I mean, this is usually our busy time of the year.

W: So those sanctions really have hurt us.
M: It looks like it. Our exports are down 12 percent over last year.

Q4. What is the problem?
　　(A) People have to stand in line.
　　(B) Production has slowed down.
　　(C) All the workers are at lunch now.
　　(D) Work has stopped completely.

Q5. What advice does the man give to the woman?
　　(A) She should be patient.
　　(B) She should hire more workers.
　　(C) She should lay off some workers.
　　(D) She should close the assembly line for a few weeks.

Q6. What is the cause of the problem?
　　(A) Strikes　　　　　　　　　(B) Cheap imports
　　(C) Sanctions　　　　　　　　(D) Illness among workers

Step 3　文法・語彙問題

空欄にふさわしい語句を選ぼう。　＜制限時間２分＞

Q7. Can I _____ a word with you about next week's meeting?
　　(A) take
　　(B) talk
　　(C) have
　　(D) make

Q8. We've had to slow _____ production for a few days.
　　(A) down
　　(B) over
　　(C) with
　　(D) for

Q9. Do you have any idea when things will be back up to _____?
　　(A) the speeds
　　(B) speeds
　　(C) speeding
　　(D) speed

Q10. Just _____ in there and don't give up.
　　(A) hope
　　(B) hang
　　(C) put
　　(D) leave

Q11. Is there any reason _____ this has happened?
　　(A) what
　　(B) where
　　(C) which
　　(D) why

Step 4　解答・解説チェック

現時点での理解度を確認しよう。

問題文は、生産ラインについて話している会話です。

1. 正解 **(B)**。質問：「話し手たちは、どこにいますか？」。答え：「職場」。ヒント：The line is really slow today.
2. 正解 **(B)**。質問：「男性は、昼食時に何をするつもりですか？」。答え：「情報を伝える」。ヒント：I was going to inform everyone at lunchtime.
3. 正解 **(A)**。質問：「昨年の輸出は、どうでしたか？」。答え：「現在よりよかった」。ヒント：Our exports are down 12 percent over last year.
4. 正解 **(B)**。質問：「何が問題になっていますか？」。答え：「生産のスピードが落ちた」。ヒント：We've had to slow down production.
5. 正解 **(A)**。質問：「男性は、女性にどんなアドバイスを与えていますか？」。答え：「我慢するように」。ヒント：Just hang in there.
6. 正解 **(C)**。質問：「問題の原因は、何ですか？」。答え：「制裁措置」。ヒント：So those sanctions really have hurt us.
7. 正解 **(C)**。文意から、have a word with「〜と話をする」を完成させる。（B）は、a word がなければ可。
8. 正解 **(A)**。slow down「〜のスピードを落とす」を完成させる。
9. 正解 **(D)**。back up to speed「（本来の）スピードを取り戻す」を完成させる。
10. 正解 **(B)**。hang in there「がんばれ」を完成させる。
11. 正解 **(D)**。文意から、reason why「〜の理由」を完成させる。

Step 5　直読直解トレーニング

速読速聴力を高めよう。
(※日本語訳は、英語の原文の順序どおりに記してあります。)

W: Nick, can I have a word with you? The line is really slow / today.
ニック、少しお話しできますか？　ラインがとても遅いです、今日は。

M: I was going to inform everyone / at lunchtime.
みんなに知らせようと思っていました、昼休みに。
We've had to slow down / production.
われわれは、落とさなければなりませんでした、生産ペースを。

W: So, any idea / when things will be back up to speed?
それで、わかりますか、いつスピードが戻るか？

M: In a few weeks. Just hang in there.
数週間のうちです。とにかくがんばりましょう。
Demand is down just a bit / right now.
需要が少し落ちています、ちょうど今。

W: Is there any reason why?
何か理由があるのですか？
I mean, this is usually our busy / time of the year.
つまり、今はいつもならいちばん忙しい時期です、1年で。

W: So / those sanctions really have hurt us.
では、それらの制裁措置が当社に本当に打撃を与えたのですね。

M: It looks like it. Our exports are down 12 percent / over last year.
そのようです。われわれの輸出は12パーセント落ちています、昨年より。

語句

slow：遅い	**inform**：～に知らせる
slow down：～のスピードを落とす	**production**：生産
back up to speed：スピードを取り戻す	**hang in there**：がんばれ
demand：需要	**sanction**：制裁
hurt：～にダメージを与える	**export**：輸出

Step 6　基本構文トレーニング
文法・語彙力を高めよう。

121	少しお話しできますか？	Can I have a word with you?
122	今日はラインがとても遅いです。	The line is really slow today.
123	昼休みに、みんなに知らせようと思っていました。	I was going to inform everyone at lunchtime.
124	われわれは、生産ペースを落とさなければなりませんでした。	We've had to slow down production.
125	スピードが戻るのは、いつだかわかりますか？	Any idea when things will be back up to speed?
126	とにかくがんばりましょう。	Just hang in there.
127	ちょうど今、需要が少し落ちています。	Demand is down just a bit right now.
128	何か理由があるのですか？	Is there any reason why?
129	今は、いつもなら1年で忙しい時期です。	This is usually our busy time of the year.
130	われわれの輸出は、昨年より12パーセント落ちています。	Our exports are down 12 percent over last year.

Day 4 説明文トレーニング

Step 1 リスニング問題
CDを聞いて、問題を解こう。＜制限時間2分＞

Q1. Who will find the information most useful?
　　(A) College students with no summer plans
　　(B) People with grown children
　　(C) Single adults wanting to make new friends
　　(D) People with young children

Q2. Which of the following is mentioned in the talk?
　　(A) Sports camps
　　(B) Mathematics camps
　　(C) Camps for learning how to drive
　　(D) Camps for learning a foreign language

Q3. Which of the following is true for camps today?
　　(A) They are too expensive for most children.
　　(B) They offer all kinds of activities.
　　(C) They mostly offer water sports.
　　(D) They are located in large cities only.

Step 2　リーディング問題

英文を読んで、問題を解こう。＜制限時間3分＞

Many kids love to try new things and make new friends in the summertime. Summer camp is a popular place to do that. These days summer camps are not just the traditional outdoor cookouts and water sports on the lake. There are many kinds of camps to choose from: computer camps, ballet camps, soccer camps, art camps, and a lot more. Even for families on a tight budget there are day camps. These are camps run mainly in urban areas. Kids at these camps go on fun field trips and they are always back home by dinnertime. So there really are summer camps out there for all types of kids.

Q4.　According to the passage, why do many kids like summer camp?
　　（A）Because it is not expensive
　　（B）Because they can get away from home
　　（C）Because they can try something new there
　　（D）Because their friends go there

Q5.　Who probably would be most interested in a day camp?
　　（A）Children who like to eat dinner at home.
　　（B）Families that do not have a lot of money.
　　（C）Parents who are worried about their children.
　　（D）Children who do not like cookouts and sports.

Q6.　What is the main point of the passage?
　　（A）There are many different kinds of camps.
　　（B）There are many kinds of children.
　　（C）Most camps are outside of urban areas.
　　（D）Most camps offer all kinds of activities.

Step 3 文法・語彙問題
空欄にふさわしい語句を選ぼう。 ＜制限時間2分＞

Q7. It is true that many kids love to try new _____.
(A) thing
(B) things
(C) something
(D) anything

Q8. They _____ new friends in the summertime, during the vacation period.
(A) do
(B) happen
(C) make
(D) occur

Q9. If you want to meet people, summer camp is a _____ place to do that.
(A) population
(B) popular
(C) popularly
(D) populated

Q10. For families _____ a tight budget there are day camps just outside the city.
(A) in
(B) at
(C) to
(D) on

Q11. They go to camps during the day but they are always back home _____ dinnertime.
(A) by
(B) until
(C) when
(D) since

Step 4　解答・解説チェック

現時点での理解度を確認しよう。

問題文は、子供たちのサマーキャンプについての話です。

1. 正解 **(D)**。質問：「この情報がもっとも役に立つのは、誰ですか？」。答え：「幼い子供がいる人」。ヒント：文書全体の内容から。
2. 正解 **(A)**。質問：「話で述べられているのは、次のどれですか？」。答え：「スポーツキャンプ」。ヒント：computer camps, ballet camps, soccer camps, art camps, and a lot more
3. 正解 **(B)**。質問：「今日のキャンプに関して、正しいのは次のどれですか？」。答え：「さまざまな種類のアクティビティを提供する」。ヒント：There are many kinds of camps.
4. 正解 **(C)**。質問：「この文書によると、多くの子供たちがサマーキャンプを好むのはなぜですか？」。答え：「そこで何か新しいことにトライできるから」。ヒント：Many kids love to try new things, Summer camp is a popular place to do that.
5. 正解 **(B)**。質問：「日帰りキャンプにもっとも興味を示すと思われるのは、誰ですか？」。答え：「お金の余裕があまりない家族」。ヒント：Even for families on a tight budget there are day camps.
6. 正解 **(A)**。質問：「この文書のいちばんのポイントは、何ですか？」。答え：「たくさんの種類のキャンプがある」。ヒント：There are many kinds of camps to choose from
7. 正解 **(B)**。文意から、new things「新しいこと」（複数形）を選ぶ。新しいことはさまざまあるので、（A）単数形は不可。
8. 正解 **(C)**。文意から、make new friends「新しい友だちを作る」を完成させる。
9. 正解 **(B)**。名詞 place「場所」の前なので、形容詞 popular「人気の」を選ぶ。(A)「人口」（名詞）、(C)「一般に」（副詞）、(D)「人口の多い」（形容詞）。
10. 正解 **(D)**。on a tight budget「厳しい予算の」を完成させる。
11. 正解 **(A)**。文意から、「（時間）までに」を意味する前置詞 by を選ぶ。

Step 5　直読直解トレーニング

速読速聴力を高めよう。

（※日本語訳は、英語の原文の順序どおりに記してあります。）

Many kids love / to try new things / and make new friends /
子供の多くは好きです、新しいことに挑戦したり、新しい友だちを作ることが、
in the summertime. Summer camp is a popular place / to do that.
夏のあいだに。サマーキャンプは人気の場所です、そうするのに。
These days / summer camps are not just / the traditional outdoor cookouts /
最近では、サマーキャンプは〜だけではありません、昔ながらの屋外での料理、
and water sports on the lake. There are many kinds of camps /
それに湖でのウォータースポーツでは。たくさんの種類のキャンプがあります、
to choose from: computer camps, ballet camps, soccer camps,
選べる。コンピュータキャンプ、バレエキャンプ、サッカーキャンプ、
art camps, and a lot more. Even for families / on a tight budget /
アートキャンプ、その他いろいろです。家族のためにも、予算が厳しい
there are day camps. These are camps / run mainly in urban areas.
日帰りキャンプがあります。これらはキャンプです、主に都市部で開催される。
Kids at these camps / go on fun field trips / and they are always back home /
これらのキャンプで子供たちは、楽しい遠足に出かけ、いつも帰宅します、
by dinnertime. So / there really are summer camps / out there /
夕食までに。ですから、サマーキャンプがあるのです、世の中には、
for all types of kids.
どのような子供たちにもあった。

語句		
traditional：伝統的な	**outdoor**：野外の	
cookout：野外料理	**ballet**：バレエ	
tight：不足している	**budget**：予算	
mainly：主として	**urban**：都市の	
field trip：遠足	**out there**：世の中には	

Step 6　基本構文トレーニング

文法・語彙力を高めよう。

131	子供たちの多くは、新しいことに挑戦することが大好きです。	Many kids love to try new things.
132	彼らは、夏のあいだに新しい友だちを作ります。	They make new friends in the summertime.
133	サマーキャンプは、そうするのに人気の場所です。	Summer camp is a popular place to do that.
134	サマーキャンプは、昔ながらの屋外での料理だけではありません。	Summer camps are not just the traditional outdoor cookouts.
135	たくさんの種類のキャンプがあります。	There are many kinds of camps.
136	予算が厳しい家族には、日帰りキャンプがあります。	For families on a tight budget there are day camps.
137	これらは、主に都市部で開催されるキャンプです。	These are camps run mainly in urban areas.
138	これらのキャンプで、子供たちは楽しい遠足に出かけます。	Kids at these camps go on fun field trips.
139	彼らは、いつも夕食までに帰宅します。	They are always back home by dinnertime.
140	どのような子供たちにもあったサマーキャンプがあります。	There are summer camps for all types of kids.

Week 3

Day 5 会話文トレーニング

Step 1 リスニング問題
CDを聞いて、問題を解こう。＜制限時間2分＞

Q1. What are the people doing?
- (A) Celebrating
- (B) Negotiating
- (C) Arguing
- (D) Exercising

Q2. How much change is the woman asking for?
- (A) Very little
- (B) None at all
- (C) Quite a lot
- (D) None except higher costs

Q3. What will probably happen soon?
- (A) The speakers will end their relationship.
- (B) The speakers will continue talking for a long time.
- (C) The speakers will start over from scratch.
- (D) The speakers will reach an agreement.

Step 2　リーディング問題

英文を読んで、問題を解こう。＜制限時間3分＞

M:　If we bend a little on this particular point, do we have a deal?
W:　I think we do, as long as you can cut costs there.

M:　Are you satisfied with everything as it is now?
W:　Pretty much. The wording needs to be changed a bit in some parts.
M:　That can easily be done.

M:　So are we agreed? Can I sign off on this deal yet?
W:　Basically, we see eye to eye. There are just a few small details left.

Q4.　What is true of the man?
　　（A）He keeps asking if the deal is satisfactory.
　　（B）He does not want to change his original offer.
　　（C）He is uncertain about what the woman wants.
　　（D）He is not very interested in making an agreement.

Q5.　What is the woman's attitude?
　　（A）She is ready to cancel the deal.
　　（B）She is satisfied with the main points.
　　（C）She agrees with everything the man has said.
　　（D）She believes some prices should be increased.

Q6.　What remains to be changed?
　　（A）Nothing
　　（B）Some minor points
　　（C）Some major points
　　（D）Almost everything

Step 3　文法・語彙問題

空欄にふさわしい語句を選ぼう。　＜制限時間2分＞

Q7. _____ a little on this particular point and we will have a deal.
- (A) Bend
- (B) Bent
- (C) Bending
- (D) Bends

Q8. You can _____ costs there if you want to save some money.
- (A) make
- (B) tear
- (C) cut
- (D) throw

Q9. Are you satisfied _____ everything as it is now?
- (A) of
- (B) for
- (C) to
- (D) with

Q10. The _____ needs to be changed a bit in this contract.
- (A) wording
- (B) working
- (C) speaking
- (D) doing

Q11. Sometimes we disagree, but basically, we see _____.
- (A) eye to eye
- (B) face to face
- (C) toe to toe
- (D) hand to hand

Step 4　解答・解説チェック

現時点での理解度を確認しよう。

問題文は、商談をまとめようと話し合っている男女の会話です。

1. 正解 **(B)**。質問：「話し手たちは、何をしていますか？」。答え：「交渉」。ヒント：do we have a deal?, So are we agreed?
2. 正解 **(A)**。質問：「女性は、どの程度の変更を求めていますか？」。答え：「ほんの少し」。ヒント：男性の If we bend a little on this particular point, 女性の I think we do.
3. 正解 **(D)**。質問：「間もなく、何が起こると思われますか？」。答え：「話し手たちが、合意に達する」。ヒント：Basically, we see eye to eye.
4. 正解 **(A)**。質問：「男性に関して、正しい記述は何ですか？」。答え：「（取引内容）が満足かを繰り返し尋ねている」。ヒント：If we bend..., do we have a deal?, Are you satisfied...?, So are we agreed?
5. 正解 **(B)**。質問：「女性の態度は、どうですか？」。答え：「主な点で満足している」。ヒント：Basically, we see eye to eye.
6. 正解 **(B)**。質問：「今後変更されることは、何ですか？」。答え：「何点かの細部」。ヒント：There are just a few small details left.
7. 正解 **(A)**。前半の節には主語がないので、動詞で始まる命令文。Bend（動詞・原形）を選び、bend (a little) on「～に関して（少し）譲歩する」を完成させる。
8. 正解 **(C)**。文意から、cut costs「コストを削減する」を完成させる。
9. 正解 **(D)**。be satisfied with「～に満足している」の疑問形を完成させる。
10. 正解 **(A)**。文意から、wording「言い回し」を選ぶ。
11. 正解 **(A)**。文意から、see eye to eye「合意している」を完成させる。

Step 5　直読直解トレーニング
速読速聴力を高めよう。
(※日本語訳は、英語の原文の順序どおりに記してあります。)

M:　If we bend a little / on this particular point, do we have a deal?
　　われわれが少し譲歩すれば、特にこの点について、交渉成立ですか？
W:　I think we do, as long as / you can cut costs there.
　　そう思います、～のであれば、その部分のコストの削減ができる。

M:　Are you satisfied / with everything / as it is now?
　　ご満足でしょうか、すべて、これで？
W:　Pretty much. The wording needs / to be changed a bit / in some parts.
　　概ね。言い回しは、必要です、多少変更が、何カ所か。
M:　That can easily be done.
　　それは簡単にできます。

M:　So / are we agreed? Can I sign off / on this deal / yet?
　　これで、合意ですか？　署名してよろしいですか、この契約に、もう？
W:　Basically, we see eye to eye. There are just a few small details / left.
　　基本的には、合意しています。2, 3 細部があるだけです、残された。

語句			
have a deal：取引が成立する		**as long as**：～さえすれば	
cut costs：コストを削減する		**as it is**：そのままに	
pretty much：かなり		**wording**：言い回し	
agreed：同意して		**sign off on**：～に署名して承認する	
see eye to eye：合意している		**details**：詳細	

Step 6　基本構文トレーニング
文法・語彙力を高めよう。

141	特にこの点について、少し譲歩してください。	Bend a little on this particular point.
142	交渉成立ですか？	Do we have a deal?
143	あなたは、その部分のコストを削減できます。	You can cut costs there.
144	これで、すべてご満足でしょうか？	Are you satisfied with everything as it is now?
145	言い回しは、多少変更が必要です。	The wording needs to be changed a bit.
146	それは簡単にできます。	That can easily be done.
147	合意ですか？	Are we agreed?
148	もう、この契約に署名してよろしいですか？	Can I sign off on this deal yet?
149	基本的には、合意しています。	Basically, we see eye to eye.
150	2, 3 細部を残すだけです。	There are just a few small details left.

Day 6 チェックテスト

ふさわしい語句の意味を選ぼう。　＜制限時間５分＞

1. glorious：(A) 好天の　(B) 気味の悪い　(C) 灰色の
2. head toward：(A) 〜に向かう　(B) 頭が痛い　(C) 〜に頭を突き出す
3. circuit：(A) 〜を切る　(B) １周　(C) 長方形
4. good sweat：(A) たっぷりの汗　(B) とても甘い
   (C) おいしいスイーツ
5. ominous：(A) 満場一致の　(B) 巨大な　(C) 不気味な
6. pick up the pace：(A) ペースを上げる　(B) ペースを落とす
   (C) ペースを確認する
7. cool off：(A) 立ち去る　(B) 考え直す　(C) 〜を涼しくする
8. thunderstorm：(A) 強風　(B) 雷雨　(C) 台風
9. cover：(A) 避難場所　(B) 向こう側　(C) 回復
10. cheat：(A) 値引く　(B) いかさまをする　(C) 〜を調べる

11. time：(A) 〜の時期を選ぶ　(B) 〜の時間を選ぶ　(C) 〜の季節を選ぶ
12. serious：(A) シリーズの　(B) 本気の　(C) 切実な
13. brand name：(A) 大きな名前　(B) ブランド品　(C) 合わせた名前
14. be prepared：(A) 備える　(B) 〜のほうを好む　(C) 予見する
15. battle it out：(A) 戦いを止める　(B) 徹底的に戦う　(C) 外で戦う
16. slash：(A) 壊れる　(B) 発疹がでる　(C) (価格を) 下げる
17. drastically：(A) 破壊的に　(B) 実践的に　(C) 大幅に
18. draw to a close：(A) 終わりに近づく　(B) 間もなく閉店する
    (C) 近くに引き寄せる
19. retail：(A) 小売りの　(B) 卸売りの　(C) 直売の
20. item：(A) 考え　(B) 商品　(C) 販売

21. slow：(A) 投げる　(B) 遅い　(C) 〜をとおして
22. inform：(A) プラットフォーム　(B) 〜を建てる　(C) 〜に知らせる

23. slow down：(A)〜を破棄する　(B)〜のスピードを落とす　(C)ゆっくり倒れる
24. production：(A)計画　(B)予算　(C)生産
25. back up to speed：(A)〜を支える　(B)スピードを取り戻す　(C)加速する
26. hang in there：(A)がんばれ　(B)止まれ　(C)そこに吊せ
27. demand：(A)需要　(B)推測　(C)在庫
28. sanction：(A)権利　(B)保護　(C)制裁
29. hurt：(A)心　(B)〜にダメージを与える　(C)〜を暖める
30. export：(A)輸出　(B)港湾　(C)取引

31. traditional：(A)伝統的な　(B)形式的な　(C)音楽的な
32. outdoor：(A)野外の　(B)開放的な　(C)外出する
33. cookout：(A)〜を調理する　(B)料理学校　(C)野外料理
34. ballet：(A)球技　(B)銃弾　(C)バレエ
35. tight：(A)ちょうどの　(B)十分な　(C)不足している
36. budget：(A)実行　(B)予算　(C)借金
37. mainly：(A)主として　(B)男性的な　(C)残る
38. urban：(A)国の　(B)都市の　(C)田舎の
39. field trip：(A)自由旅行　(B)遠足　(C)帰郷
40. out there：(A)足元に　(B)野外に　(C)世の中には

41. have a deal：(A)取引が成立する　(B)取引を破棄する　(C)取引が頓挫する
42. as long as：(A)〜ほど長く　(B)〜と同じくらい長く　(C)〜さえすれば
43. cut costs：(A)コストを計算する　(B)コストを削減する　(C)コストを見直す
44. as it is：(A)そのままに　(B)もうすぐ　(C)そうであれば
45. pretty much：(A)とてもかわいい　(B)あまり〜でない　(C)かなり
46. wording：(A)敬語　(B)言い回し　(C)作詞
47. agreed：(A)あいさつして　(B)同意して　(C)決裂して

48. sign off on：(A) 〜に署名して承認する　(B) 〜を拒否する　(C) 〜を削除する
49. see eye to eye：(A) にらみ合う　(B) 対立している　(C) 合意している
50. details：(A) 詳細　(B) 取引　(C) 交渉

チェックテスト解答

1. **(A)**	2. **(A)**	3. **(B)**	4. **(A)**	5. **(C)**
6. **(A)**	7. **(C)**	8. **(B)**	9. **(A)**	10. **(B)**
11. **(A)**	12. **(B)**	13. **(B)**	14. **(A)**	15. **(B)**
16. **(C)**	17. **(C)**	18. **(A)**	19. **(A)**	20. **(B)**
21. **(B)**	22. **(C)**	23. **(B)**	24. **(C)**	25. **(B)**
26. **(A)**	27. **(A)**	28. **(C)**	29. **(B)**	30. **(A)**
31. **(A)**	32. **(A)**	33. **(C)**	34. **(C)**	35. **(C)**
36. **(B)**	37. **(A)**	38. **(B)**	39. **(B)**	40. **(C)**
41. **(A)**	42. **(C)**	43. **(B)**	44. **(A)**	45. **(C)**
46. **(B)**	47. **(B)**	48. **(A)**	49. **(C)**	50. **(A)**

＜ワンポイント＞

　第3週のトレーニングはいかがでしたか？　ナチュラルスピードのリスニングに慣れてきましたか？　少し耳がなじんできた気がしたら、「リラックスして聞く」ことができ始めている証拠です。でも、耳はなじんできたけれど、「リーディングでは、知らない単語が多くて理解できない」という方も多いはずです。

　実は、リーディング上達のコツは、「知らない単語は無視すること」です。リスニングでは、知らない単語は聞き取れませんから、自然に無視しているのですが、リーディングでは、知らない単語が目に飛び込んできてしまいます。これを無視して、目を先に進めることがポイントです。

　もちろん、復習の際に、知らない単語の意味を確認するのはいいことですが、問題を解く際に気にするのはNGです。知らない単語に意識を向けるのではなく、知っている単語から想像しましょう。リスニング力同様、リーディング力も想像力です。

第5章

Week 4

Week 4
今週のトレーニング

Day 1〜 Day 5 のトレーニング			
Step	内容		時間
1	リスニング問題（3問）		2分
2	リーディング問題（3問）		3分
3	文法・語彙問題（5問）		2分
4	解答・解説チェック		3分
5	直読直解トレーニング		5〜15分
	①	CD（英語）を聞いて、英文を目で追う。	
	②	CD（英語）を聞いて、日本語訳を目で追う。	
	③	カンマ (,)、ピリオド (.)、スラッシュ (/) の単位で、英文の意味が理解できるか確認（理解できない部分は、日本語訳や語彙を参照）。	
6	基本構文トレーニング		5〜15分
	①	1文ずつCD（日本語・英語）を聞き、英語を数回音読。	
	②	10文の英語を続けて音読（数回行なう）。	
	③	テキストを縦に半分に折るなどして日本語訳を隠し、英語部分を見て意味がすぐにわかるか確認。	
	④	応用トレーニング「ルックアップ＆セイ」「音読筆写」「リピーティング」	

<ワンポイント>

　移動中などに、音声CDを使って「基本構文のシャドウイング」（12ページ）を、試してみましたか？　うまくできないという方は、応用トレーニングに「リピーティング」を加えると、シャドウイングが楽になるはずです。

リピーティング	基本構文（日→英）を聞き、英語のあとで一時停止して、何も見ずに聞き取った英語を話します。

Week 4

Day 1 会話文トレーニング

Step 1 リスニング問題
CDを聞いて、問題を解こう。＜制限時間2分＞

Q1. Where will these people go sometime in the future?
　　(A) To a desert
　　(B) To the ocean
　　(C) To the mountains
　　(D) To a large city

Q2. How has the weather been recently?
　　(A) It has rained.
　　(B) It has snowed.
　　(C) There has been an ice storm.
　　(D) There has been a heat wave.

Q3. What is the man interested in doing?
　　(A) Learning to snowboard
　　(B) Going skiing
　　(C) Meeting Julie in marketing
　　(D) Getting away from the cold weather

Step 2　リーディング問題

英文を読んで、問題を解こう。＜制限時間 3 分＞

M: Can you believe how cold it's been? Winter has certainly come early this year.
W: The only good thing is, the slopes should have some nice powder.

M: You ski a lot, do you?
W: No, I snowboard. I tried skiing a couple of times but I just couldn't get into it.
M: Can you do tricks and things like that on your snowboard?

M: Wow, you'd actually teach me? I've always wanted to learn how to snowboard.
W: Sure. Come on up with us sometime this season. You know Julie in marketing also snowboards, too.

Q4. What is the main topic of this conversation?
　　(A) Teaching　　　　　　　(B) Marketing
　　(C) The weather　　　　　 (D) A winter sport

Q5. Who knows how to snowboard?
　　(A) The man and Julie　　　(B) The woman and Julie
　　(C) The woman and the man　(D) The man, the woman, and Julie

Q6. What does the woman offer to do?
　　(A) Introduce the man to Julie
　　(B) Go skiing with the man and Julie
　　(C) Show the man how to do something
　　(D) Explain to the man where the slopes are

Step 3 文法・語彙問題

空欄にふさわしい語句を選ぼう。 ＜制限時間2分＞

Q7. Can you believe _____ cold it's been this year?
   (A) that
   (B) such
   (C) what
   (D) how

Q8. The _____ should have some nice powder for good skiing.
   (A) slopes
   (B) paths
   (C) highs
   (D) ups

Q9. I tried to learn to ski, but I just couldn't get _____ it.
   (A) in
   (B) into
   (C) over
   (D) above

Q10. You know, I've always _____ to learn how to snowboard.
   (A) want
   (B) wanted
   (C) wanting
   (D) have wanted

Q11. Come on up with us _____ this season when we go skiing.
   (A) something
   (B) anyone
   (C) anything
   (D) sometime

Step 4　解答・解説チェック

現時点での理解度を確認しよう。

問題文は、ウインター・スポーツの話をする男女の会話です。

1. 正解 **(C)**。質問：「話し手たちは、近々どこに行きますか？」。答え：「山」。ヒント：スノーボードの話と、Come on up with us sometime this season から。
2. 正解 **(B)**。質問：「最近の天気は、どうでしたか？」。答え：「雪が降っていた」。ヒント：the slopes should have some nice powder.
3. 正解 **(A)**。質問：「男性は、何をすることに興味を持っていますか？」。答え：「スノーボードを習うこと」。ヒント：I've always wanted to learn how to snowboard.
4. 正解 **(D)**。質問：「この会話の主たる話題は、何ですか？」。答え：「ウインター・スポーツ」。ヒント：ski, snowboard
5. 正解 **(B)**。質問：「スノーボードの乗り方を知っているのは、誰ですか？」。答え：「女性とジュリー」。ヒント：No, I snowboard., You know Julie in marketing also snowboards, too.
6. 正解 **(C)**。質問：「女性は、何をすることを申し出ましたか？」。答え：「男性に何かをやってみせる」。ヒント：Wow, you'd actually teach me?, Sure.
7. 正解 **(D)**。文意から、how cold it's been「（これまで）いかに寒かったか」を完成させる。
8. 正解 **(A)**。文意から、slopes「ゲレンデ」（複数形）を選ぶ。
9. 正解 **(B)**。get into「～に夢中になる」の否定文を完成させる。
10. 正解 **(B)**。I've = I have から、現在完了形にするために wanted を選ぶ。
11. 正解 **(D)**。sometime「いつか」を選び、sometime this season「今シーズンのいつか」を完成させる。

Step 5 直読直解トレーニング
速読速聴力を高めよう。
(※日本語訳は、英語の原文の順序どおりに記してあります。)

M: Can you believe / how cold it's been?
    信じられません、このところの寒さを。
    Winter has certainly come early / this year.
    冬が確かに早く来ました、今年は。
W: The only good thing is, the slopes should have some nice powder.
    唯一のいいことは、斜面にいい粉雪が積もっていることです。

M: You ski a lot, do you?
    よくスキーをするのですね？
W: No, I snowboard.
    いいえ、スノーボードをします。
    I tried skiing / a couple of times / but I just couldn't get into it.
    スキーをやってみました、2回ほど、しかし好きになれませんでした。
M: Can you do tricks and things like that / on your snowboard?
    技とかもできるのですか、スノーボードで？

M: Wow, you'd actually teach me?
    わーぁ、私に本当に教えてくれるのですか？
    I've always wanted to learn / how to snowboard.
    ずっと習いたいと思っていました、スノーボードのやり方を。
W: Sure. Come on up with us / sometime this season.
    もちろん。私たちと一緒に行きましょう、今シーズンのいつか。
    You know / Julie in marketing also snowboards, too.
    ほら、マーケティング部のジュリーもスノーボードをします。

語句
believe：〜を信じる　**certainly**：確かに　**slope**：斜面　**powder**：粉
ski：スキーをする　**get into**：〜に夢中になる　**do tricks**：芸当をする
like that：そのような　**Sure.**：もちろん　**marketing**：販売促進活動

Step 6　基本構文トレーニング

文法・語彙力を高めよう。

151	このところの寒さを信じられません。	Can you believe how cold it's been?
152	今年は、冬が確かに早く来ました。	Winter has certainly come early this year.
153	斜面に、いい粉雪が積もっているはずです。	The slopes should have some nice powder.
154	よくスキーをするのですね？	You ski a lot, do you?
155	2回ほど、スキーをやってみました。	I tried skiing a couple of times.
156	それを好きになれませんでした。	I just couldn't get into it.
157	スノーボードで、技をできるのですか？	Can you do tricks on your snowboard?
158	私に本当に教えてくれるのですか？	You'd actually teach me?
159	ずっとスノーボードのやり方を習いたいと思っていました。	I've always wanted to learn how to snowboard.
160	今シーズンのいつか、私たちと一緒に行きましょう。	Come on up with us sometime this season.

Week 4

Day 2 説明文トレーニング

Step 1 リスニング問題

CD を聞いて、問題を解こう。＜制限時間 2 分＞

Q1. How is horse racing in India described?
　　(A) It is different from what most people expect.
　　(B) It is much like horse racing everywhere else in the world.
　　(C) It is dangerous.
　　(D) It is boring.

Q2. What do local people wear to horse races in India?
　　(A) Casual clothes
　　(B) Fancy clothes
　　(C) Masks of famous people's faces
　　(D) Shirts with pictures on them

Q3. Which of these could be seen at an Indian horse race?
　　(A) A political debate
　　(B) An eating contest
　　(C) A cricket match
　　(D) A fashion show

Step 2　リーディング問題

英文を読んで、問題を解こう。＜制限時間 3 分＞

Spend a day at the races in India and you'll experience something unusual. You'll find that it's unlike visiting a horse racetrack in most countries. First of all, there's a dress code. Men would never be seen in shorts and T-shirts. It's strictly jacket and tie. Women dress up, too, in their finest fashionable dresses. Summer hats are also sported by many of these stylish women. You may even think that some of those women look like fashion models— and they are! Some racetracks have fashion shows in the middle of the day.

Q4. What is one of the unusual things about horse racing in India?
　　(A) The races last a whole day.
　　(B) The horses wear something special.
　　(C) People dress up to attend the races.
　　(D) People attend only in warmer weather.

Q5. Which of these probably would not be worn to an Indian racetrack?
　　(A) Tennis shoes
　　(B) Summer hats
　　(C) Stylish dresses
　　(D) Jackets and ties

Q6. What is said about models at horse races?
　　(A) They always attend.
　　(B) They are among those who attend.
　　(C) They are the only women who attend.
　　(D) They can attend only some of the races.

Step 3　文法・語彙問題
空欄にふさわしい語句を選ぼう。　＜制限時間2分＞

Q7. You'll experience _____ unusual if you go to the races there.
  (A) a thing
  (B) something
  (C) any
  (D) some

Q8. There's a _____ code that most people follow.
  (A) shirt
  (B) suit
  (C) dress
  (D) clothes

Q9. Men would never _____ in shorts and T-shirts at such an event.
  (A) see
  (B) be seen
  (C) be seeing
  (D) seen

Q10. To go to the races, women dress up _____ their finest fashionable dresses.
  (A) of (B) on
  (C) in (D) for

Q11. Some of those women _____ like fashion models, and they are models.
  (A) see
  (B) look
  (C) display
  (D) resemble

Step 4　解答・解説チェック

現時点での理解度を確認しよう。

問題文は、インドの競馬場の風景についての話です。

1. 正解 **(A)**。質問:「インドでの競馬は、どのように説明されていますか？」。答え:「ほとんどの人が想像しているのとは異なる」。ヒント: Spend a day at the races in India and you'll experience something unusual.
2. 正解 **(B)**。質問:「インドの人びとは競馬場に行く時に、どんな服を着ますか？」。答え:「おしゃれな服」。ヒント: It's strictly jacket and tie., Women dress up, too, in their finest fashionable dresses.
3. 正解 **(D)**。質問:「インドの競馬で目にすることができるのは、次のどれですか？」。答え:「ファッションショー」。ヒント: Some racetracks have fashion shows
4. 正解 **(C)**。質問:「インドの競馬で普通と異なることの1つは、何ですか？」。答え:「人びとが競馬場に行く時にドレスアップする」。ヒント: Women dress up, too,
5. 正解 **(A)**。質問:「インドの競馬場ではおそらく身に付けていないと思われるのは、次のどれですか？」。答え:「テニスシューズ」。ヒント: Men would never be seen in shorts and T-shirts., It's strictly jacket and tie. Women dress up, too,
6. 正解 **(B)**。質問:「競馬場でのファッションモデルに関して、どんなことが述べられていますか？」。答え:「観客の中にいる」。ヒント: some of those women look like fashion models—and they are!
7. 正解 **(B)**。something unusual「普通とは違う何か」を完成させる。
8. 正解 **(C)**。dress code「服装規定」を完成させる。
9. 正解 **(B)**。in shorts and T-shirts「短パンにTシャツでいる（ところ）」から、never be seen「決して見られることはない」(受動態) を完成させる。
10. 正解 **(C)**。前置詞 in「～を着用して」を選び、in their finest fashionable dresses「（自分が持っている中で）いちばんの流行のドレスで」を完成させる。
11. 正解 **(B)**。Some of those women の様子を伝える文意から、look like「～のように見える」を完成させる。

Step 5　直読直解トレーニング

速読速聴力を高めよう。
（※日本語訳は、英語の原文の順序どおりに記してあります。）

Spend a day / at the races in India / and you'll experience /
1日過ごしてください、インドの競馬場で、すると経験するでしょう、
something unusual. You'll find / that it's unlike visiting a horse racetrack /
少し変わったことを。気づくでしょう、それは競馬場に行くのとは違うことに
in most countries. First of all, there's a dress code.
たいていの国で。まず、ドレスコードがあります。
Men would never be seen / in shorts and T-shirts.
男性を目にすることは決してありません、短パンとTシャツの。
It's strictly jacket and tie.
必ずジャケットにネクタイです。
Women dress up, too, in their finest fashionable dresses.
女性もドレスアップしています、すばらしい流行のドレスで。
Summer hats are also sported / by many of these stylish women.
夏用の帽子も、上品に着用されます、多くのこうしたおしゃれな女性によって。
You may even think / that some of those women / look like fashion models /
思うことさえあります、女性の何人かは、ファッションモデルのようだと、
—and they are! Some racetracks / have fashion shows /
彼女らは、そうなのです！　競馬場もあります、ファッションショーを行なう、
in the middle of the day.
日中に。

語句		
	experience：〜を経験する	**unlike**：〜とは異なって
	horse racetrack：競馬場	**first of all**：まず始めに
	dress code：服装規定	**strictly**：絶対に
	dress up：めかし込む	**fashionable**：流行の
	sport：〜を上品に着こなす	**stylish**：おしゃれな

Step 6　基本構文トレーニング

文法・語彙力を高めよう。

CD 68

161	競馬場で1日過ごしてください。	Spend a day at the races.
162	少し変わったことを経験するでしょう。	You'll experience something unusual.
163	それは、たいていの国で競馬場に行くのとは違います。	It's unlike visiting a horse racetrack in most countries.
164	ドレスコードがあります。	There's a dress code.
165	短パンとTシャツの男性を目にすることは決してありません。	Men would never be seen in shorts and T-shirts.
166	必ずジャケットにネクタイです。	It's strictly jacket and tie.
167	女性は、すばらしい流行のドレスで、ドレスアップしています。	Women dress up in their finest fashionable dresses.
168	夏用の帽子も上品に着用されます。	Summer hats are also sported.
169	それらの女性の何人かは、ファッションモデルのようです。	Some of those women look like fashion models.
170	ファッションショーを行なう競馬場もあります。	Some racetracks have fashion shows.

Day 3　会話文トレーニング

Step 1　リスニング問題
CDを聞いて、問題を解こう。＜制限時間2分＞

Q1. Where are the speakers?
   (A) In an office
   (B) In a store
   (C) In a park
   (D) In a classroom

Q2. What is true of the speakers?
   (A) They are members of the same family.
   (B) They work together.
   (C) They do not know each other.
   (D) They share an apartment.

Q3. What does the woman think the cashier will do?
   (A) Tell the man to leave
   (B) Hit the man
   (C) Refund her money
   (D) Agree with her

Step 2　リーディング問題

英文を読んで、問題を解こう。＜制限時間3分＞

M: Excuse me, Miss. Miss! Excuse me! There's a line, you know.
W: Miss? Who are you calling "Miss"? It's Ms., and I am in line.

M: OK, Ms., I'm sorry to have to point this out, but the line starts back there.
W: No, it doesn't. It starts to the left of the register. See that sign, Mister?
M: See all these people behind me? I think you're wrong.

M: OK, let's ask this cashier here. Whatever she says we'll agree to. OK?
W: Agreed, but she'll say I'm right, so I don't know why we're even asking her.

Q4. Where are these two people?
　　(A) In a store　　　　　　(B) At school
　　(C) In an office　　　　　(D) At a bus stop

Q5. What are the man and woman doing?
　　(A) Joking
　　(B) Chatting
　　(C) Gossiping
　　(D) Disagreeing

Q6. What will happen next, right after this dialogue?
　　(A) They will leave.
　　(B) They will ask someone a question.
　　(C) The man will move to another line.
　　(D) The woman will get in line behind the man.

Step 3　文法・語彙問題

空欄にふさわしい語句を選ぼう。　＜制限時間2分＞

Q7. I am _____ line, so don't tell me what to do.
   (A) in
   (B) at
   (C) to
   (D) of

Q8. The line doesn't start there; it starts to the left of the _____.
   (A) cash
   (B) cashing
   (C) registration
   (D) register

Q9. Let's _____ this cashier here and we'll see who's right.
   (A) say
   (B) speak
   (C) ask
   (D) guess

Q10. I don't know who's right, but whatever she says we'll _____ to.
   (A) agreement
   (B) agree
   (C) agreed
   (D) agreeing

Q11. I don't know why we're _____ asking her, because I know I'm right.
   (A) such
   (B) so
   (C) even
   (D) much

Step 4　解答・解説チェック

現時点での理解度を確認しよう。

問題文は、順番待ちの列での男女の会話です。

1. 正解 **(B)**。質問：「話し手たちは、どこにいますか？」。答え：「店の中」。ヒント：It starts to the left of the register.
2. 正解 **(C)**。質問：「話し手たちに関して、正しいことは何ですか？」。答え：「おたがいを知らない」。ヒント：Excuse me, Miss.
3. 正解 **(D)**。質問：「女性は、レジ係がどうすると思っていますか？」。答え：「彼女に同意する」。ヒント：she'll say I'm right
4. 正解 **(A)**。質問：「この2人は、どこにいますか？」。答え：「店の中」。ヒント：Q1 同様。
5. 正解 **(D)**。質問：「男性と女性は、どうしていますか？」。答え：「意見が食い違っている」。ヒント：会話の流れ全般から。
6. 正解 **(B)**。質問：「この会話が終了した直後に、何が起こりますか？」。答え：「誰かに質問する」。ヒント：let's ask this cashier here
7. 正解 **(A)**。文意から、I am in line「私は列に並んでいる」を完成させる。
8. 正解 **(D)**。文意から、register「レジ」を選ぶ。(A)「現金」、(B)「現金化」、(C)「登録」。
9. 正解 **(C)**。ask「(人) に尋ねる」を選び、let's ask「(人) に聞いてみましょう」を完成させる。
10. 正解 **(B)**。助動詞 will のあとなので、動詞の原形がくる。agree to「～に同意する」を完成させる。
11. 正解 **(C)**。文意から、動詞を強調する even を選び、even ask「あえて、(人) に尋ねる」の現在進行形を完成させる。

Step 5　直読直解トレーニング
速読速聴力を高めよう。
（※日本語訳は、英語の原文の順序どおりに記してあります。）

M:　Excuse me, Miss. Miss! Excuse me! There's a line, you know.
　　もしもし、お嬢さん。お嬢さん！　すみません！　並んでいるんですよ。
W:　Miss? Who are you calling "Miss"? It's Ms., and I am in line.
　　お嬢さん？　「お嬢さん」って誰？　私は「ミズ」、そして並んでいます。

M:　OK, Ms., I'm sorry to have to point this out,
　　わかりました、ミズ、こんなことを言ってすみませんが、
　　but the line starts back there.
　　列は、うしろから始まっています。
W:　No, it doesn't. It starts / to the left of the register.
　　いいえ、違います。それは始まっています、レジの左から。
　　See that sign, Mister?
　　あのサインが見えませんか、ミスター？
M:　See all these people behind me? I think / you're wrong.
　　私のうしろの人たちが見えませんか？　思います、あなたが間違っていると。

M:　OK, let's ask this cashier here.
　　わかりました、ここのレジ係に聞きましょう。
　　Whatever she says / we'll agree to. OK?
　　彼女がなんと言っても、われわれは、従いましょう。いいですか？
W:　Agreed, but she'll say I'm right, so I don't know /
　　いいです、でも彼女は私が正しいと言うでしょう、だからわかりません
　　why we're even asking her.
　　なぜわれわれはあえて彼女に聞くのか。

語句

in line：列に並んで　**point out**：〜を指摘する　**back there**：後方のそこ
to the left：左側に　**register**：レジ　**sign**：標示　**behind**：〜のうしろに
cashier：レジ係　**whatever**：何でも　**agree to**：〜に同意する

Step 6　基本構文トレーニング
文法・語彙力を高めよう。

171	「お嬢さん」って誰のことですか？	Who are you calling "Miss"?
172	私は、並んでいます。	I am in line.
173	列は、うしろから始まっています。	The line starts back there.
174	それは、レジの左から始まっています。	It starts to the left of the register.
175	私のうしろの人たちが見えませんか？	See all these people behind me?
176	あなたは間違っていると思います。	I think you're wrong.
177	ここのレジ係に聞きましょう。	Let's ask this cashier here.
178	彼女がなんと言っても、われわれは従いましょう。	Whatever she says we'll agree to.
179	彼女は、私が正しいと言うでしょう。	She'll say I'm right.
180	なぜわれわれは、あえて彼女に聞くのかわかりません。	I don't know why we're even asking her.

Day 4 説明文トレーニング

Step 1 リスニング問題
CDを聞いて、問題を解こう。＜制限時間2分＞

Q1. According to the speaker, what has increased?
- (A) Rentals of PVRs
- (B) Sales of box sets of DVDs
- (C) Commercials on TV programs
- (D) Viewing of dramas and sitcoms

Q2. Which of the following does the speaker explain?
- (A) Why more people are going to the theater
- (B) Why more people are renting DVDs
- (C) Why more people are seeing live performances
- (D) Why more people are buying large-screen television sets

Q3. According to the speaker, what do some people dislike about television?
- (A) The bad language
- (B) The violence
- (C) The poor quality
- (D) The commercials

Step 2 リーディング問題

英文を読んで、問題を解こう。＜制限時間3分＞

TV ratings are down across the board for most dramas and sitcoms, yet DVD rentals and purchases of those same TV shows are way up. What's going on here? Basically, what's happening is a revolution in how TV shows are viewed. Many families are too busy now to watch TV shows at the regular times. They may even be too lazy to record them with their VCRs or PVRs. One reason DVD box sets are such a hit is the absence of commercials; another big reason is the great picture quality. Also, there is the fact that you can watch episodes back to back at your leisure. That's a huge plus.

Q4. How does the passage describe DVDs?
   (A) They are educational.
   (B) They are cheap.
   (C) They are convenient.
   (D) They are complicated.

Q5. Why are some people purchasing sets of DVDs?
   (A) They are easy to store.
   (B) They are not expensive.
   (C) They are available everywhere.
   (D) They have no advertising on them.

Q6. What do VCRs and PVRs have in common?
   (A) Their prices are way down now.
   (B) They can be played back to back.
   (C) They have replaced regular TV sets.
   (D) Both are used for recording TV programs.

Step 3　文法・語彙問題

空欄にふさわしい語句を選ぼう。　＜制限時間２分＞

Q7. TV ratings are down _____ the board for most dramas and sitcoms.
   (A) over
   (B) under
   (C) above
   (D) across

Q8. At the same time, DVD rentals of those _____ TV shows are way up.
   (A) equal
   (B) same
   (C) even
   (D) like

Q9. Many families are _____ busy now to watch TV at the regular times.
   (A) too
   (B) such
   (C) over
   (D) that

Q10. As for their popularity, one reason is the _____ of commercials.
   (A) absent
   (B) absence
   (C) disappear
   (D) disappeared

Q11. With DVDs, you can watch episodes _____ at your leisure.
   (A) front to front
   (B) stop to go
   (C) back to back
   (D) open to close

Step 4　解答・解説チェック

現時点での理解度を確認しよう。

問題文は、テレビ番組の新しい見られ方についての話です。

1. 正解**(B)**。質問：「話し手によると、何が増加していますか？」。答え：「ボックス入りのセットDVDの売上」。ヒント：One reason DVD box sets are such a hit
2. 正解 **(B)**。質問：「話し手が説明しているのは、次のどれですか？」。答え：「これまでより多くの人が、DVDをレンタルする理由」。ヒント：Many families are 以下。
3. 正解 **(D)**。質問：「話し手によると、一部の人が嫌うのはテレビの何ですか？」。答え：「コマーシャル」。ヒント：One reason DVD box sets are such a hit is the absence of commercials
4. 正解 **(C)**。質問：「文書は、DVDをどのように説明していますか？」。答え：「便利である」。ヒント：You can watch episodes back to back at your leisure
5. 正解 **(D)**。質問：「ある人びとは、なぜセットDVDを購入しているのですか？」。答え：「コマーシャルが入っていないから」。ヒント：One reason DVD box sets are such a hit is the absence of commercials
6. 正解 **(D)**。質問：「VCRとPVRに共通なことは、何ですか？」。答え：「どちらもテレビ番組の録画に使われる」。ヒント：They may even be too lazy to record them with their VCRs or PVRs.
7. 正解 **(D)**。文意から、across the board「全般にわたって」を完成させる。
8. 正解 **(B)**。文意から、same「同じ」を選ぶ。（A）は、「平等な」で不可。
9. 正解 **(A)**。形容詞 busy「忙しい」を修飾する副詞 too を選び、too busy to + 動詞「〜するには忙しすぎる」を完成させる。
10. 正解 **(B)**。文意から、the absence of「〜がないこと」を完成させる。
11. 正解 **(C)**。文意から、back to back「連続して」を完成させる。

Step 5　直読直解トレーニング
速読速聴力を高めよう。
(※日本語訳は、英語の原文の順序どおりに記してあります。)

TV ratings are down / across the board / for most dramas and sitcoms,
テレビの視聴率は下がっています、全般に、多くのドラマやホームコメディで、
yet DVD rentals and purchases / of those same TV shows are / way up.
しかしレンタル DVD や購入は、同じテレビ番組の、大きく伸びています。
What's going on here? Basically, what's happening is a revolution /
これは何が起きているのでしょうか？　基本的に、起きていることは変革です、
in how TV shows are viewed. Many families are / too busy now to watch /
テレビ番組の見られ方の。多くの家庭は、忙しすぎて今や見ることができません、
TV shows / at the regular times. They may even be /
テレビ番組を、決められた放映時間に。彼らは〜のかもさえしれません、
too lazy to record / them / with their VCRs or PVRs. One reason /
不精すぎて録画できない、それらを、VCR や PVR で。理由の１つは、
DVD box sets are such a hit / is the absence of commercials;
DVD セットがこれほど人気を集めている、コマーシャルがないことです。
another big reason / is the great picture quality. Also, there is the fact /
もう１つの大きな理由は、すばらしい画質です。それに、事実があります、
that you can watch episodes back to back / at your leisure.
何話も続けて見ることができるという、暇な時に。
That's a huge plus.
それは大きな利点です。

語句

- **across the board**：全般にわたって
- **purchase**：購入
- **revolution**：革命
- **lazy**：怠慢な
- **back to back**：連続して
- **sitcom**：ホームコメディ
- **way**：はるかに
- **regular**：いつもの
- **absence**：不在
- **leisure**：余暇

Step 6　基本構文トレーニング

文法・語彙力を高めよう。

181	テレビの視聴率は、全般に下がっています。	TV ratings are down across the board.
182	同じテレビ番組のレンタル DVD は大きく伸びています。	DVD rentals of those same TV shows are way up.
183	これは何が起きているのでしょうか？	What's going on here?
184	それは、テレビ番組の見られ方の変革です。	It's a revolution in how TV shows are viewed.
185	今や多くの家庭は忙しすぎます。	Many families are too busy now.
186	彼らは、不精すぎて、それらを録画できないのかもしれません。	They may be too lazy to record them.
187	理由の1つは、コマーシャルがないことです。	One reason is the absence of commercials.
188	もう1つの大きな理由は、すばらしい画質です。	Another big reason is the great picture quality.
189	何話も続けて見ることができます。	You can watch episodes back to back.
190	それは大きな利点です。	That's a huge plus.

Week 4

Day 5　会話文トレーニング

Step 1　リスニング問題
CD を聞いて、問題を解こう。＜制限時間 2 分＞

Q1. Where are the people?
　　(A) In a room that is nearly empty.
　　(B) In a room filled with people.
　　(C) In a room filled with old things.
　　(D) In a room that is neat and clean.

Q2. What are the people doing?
　　(A) Playing with old toys
　　(B) Shopping in an antiques store
　　(C) Deciding what to do with some things
　　(D) Viewing an unusual exhibition in a museum

Q3. Why does the man not want to throw away the comic books?
　　(A) He wants to pass them on to his children.
　　(B) He loves to read.
　　(C) He collects all sorts of old things.
　　(D) He thinks they are valuable.

Step 2　リーディング問題
英文を読んで、問題を解こう。＜制限時間3分＞

M: Where shall we start? There's so much junk in here.
W: You can start with those boxes over there. I'll go through these drawers.

M: Diana, can we toss these old toys out? They all look like they've seen better days.
W: You can decide which ones to keep. How about this pile of car magazines?
M: Yeah, those can all go, but don't throw out the comic books. They're worth something.

M: This pile here can go to charity rather than throwing them out.
W: Then that pile over by the bikes is ... what exactly?

Q4. What is clear about the man and woman?
　　(A) They are at home.
　　(B) They have children.
　　(C) They are collectors.
　　(D) They have just begun.

Q5. What does the man want to keep?
　　(A) A bike　　　　　　　　(B) Some toys
　　(C) Comic books　　　　　(D) Car magazines

Q6. What is the woman puzzled about?
　　(A) Where to start cleaning up
　　(B) Where the toys came from
　　(C) What is in the pile by the bikes
　　(D) What should be given to charity

Step 3　文法・語彙問題

空欄にふさわしい語句を選ぼう。　＜制限時間２分＞

Q7.　There's so much _____ in here, I don't know where to start.
- (A) junking
- (B) junky
- (C) junk
- (D) junks

Q8.　You can start with those boxes _____ there in the corner.
- (A) on
- (B) at
- (C) with
- (D) over

Q9.　While you do that, I'll go through these _____.
- (A) drawer
- (B) drawers
- (C) draws
- (D) drawing

Q10.　Can we _____ these old toys out, or should we keep them?
- (A) make
- (B) burn
- (C) toss
- (D) trash

Q11.　They're old, and they all look like they've seen better _____.
- (A) days
- (B) hours
- (C) weeks
- (D) months

Step 4　解答・解説チェック

現時点での理解度を確認しよう。

問題文は、古い物の整理を始めた男女の会話です。

1. 正解 **(C)**。質問:「話し手たちは、どこにいますか?」。答え:「古い物でいっぱいの部屋」。ヒント: There's so much junk in here.
2. 正解 **(C)**。質問:「話し手たちは、何をしていますか?」。答え:「ある物をどうするか決めている」。ヒント: can we toss these old toys out?, You can decide which ones to keep.
3. 正解 **(D)**。質問:「男性は、なぜ漫画を捨てたくないのですか?」。答え:「価値があると思っている」。ヒント: don't throw out the comic books. They're worth something.
4. 正解 **(D)**。質問:「男性と女性について明らかなことは、何ですか?」。答え:「始めたところ」。ヒント: Where shall we start?, I'll go through these drawers.
5. 正解 **(C)**。質問:「男性が取っておきたい物は、何ですか?」。答え:「コミック本」。ヒント: don't throw out the comic books.
6. 正解 **(C)**。質問:「女性は、何に困惑していますか?」。答え:「自転車のそばの山が何か」。ヒント: that pile over by the bikes is ... what exactly?
7. 正解 **(C)**。much のあとなので、不可算名詞がくる。junk「ガラクタ」を選ぶ。(B)「ガラクタの」(形容詞)。(D) の用法はない。
8. 正解 **(D)**。文意から、over there「あそこ」を完成させる。
9. 正解 **(B)**。this (指示代名詞) の複数形 these のあとなので、drawers「引出し」(複数形) を選ぶ。
10. 正解 **(C)**。文意から、or 以下の後半の節の動詞 keep「~を取っておく」の反対の意味にするために、toss ~ out「~を放り出す」を完成させる。
11. 正解 **(A)**。days を選び、have seen better days「古くて使えなくなった」を完成させる。

Step 5　直読直解トレーニング

速読速聴力を高めよう。
（※日本語訳は、英語の原文の順序どおりに記してあります。）

M: Where shall we start? There's so much junk in here.
どこから始めましょうか？　ここには、ずいぶんガラクタがあります。

W: You can start / with those boxes over there.
あなたは始めてもいいですよ、あそこの箱から。
I'll go through these drawers.
私はこれらの引出しを片づけます。

M: Diana, can we toss these old toys out?
ダイアナ、これらの古いおもちゃを捨てていいですか？
They all look like / they've seen better days.
それらはすべて〜ようです、御用済みの。

W: You can decide / which ones to keep.
あなたが決めてかまいません、どれを残すかは。
How about / this pile of car magazines?
どうですか、この自動車雑誌の山は？

M: Yeah, those can all go, but don't throw out the comic books.
ええ、それらは全部捨てていいです、しかし漫画本は捨てないでください。
They're worth something.
それらは多少の価値があります。

M: This pile here can go to charity / rather than throwing them out.
ここのこの山はチャリティーに出せます、それらを捨てるよりも。

W: Then / that pile over / by the bikes is ... what exactly?
それから、あそこのあの山は、自転車のそばの、一体何ですか？

語句

junk：ガラクタ　**go through**：〜を終わらせる　**drawer**：引出し
toss out：〜を放り出す　**have seen better days**：使い古された　**decide**：〜を決定する
pile：積み重ね　**throw out**：〜を捨てる　**worth**：〜の価値がある
rather than：〜よりむしろ

Step 6　基本構文トレーニング
文法・語彙力を高めよう。

191	どこから始めましょうか？	Where shall we start?
192	ここには、ずいぶんガラクタがあります。	There's so much junk in here.
193	あなたは、あそこの箱から始めてもいいですよ。	You can start with those boxes over there.
194	私は、これらの引出しを片づけます。	I'll go through these drawers.
195	これらの古いおもちゃは捨てていいですか？	Can we toss these old toys out?
196	それらはすべて、御用済みのようです。	They all look like they've seen better days.
197	どれを残すかは、あなたが決めてかまいません。	You can decide which ones to keep.
198	この自動車雑誌の山はどうですか？	How about this pile of car magazines?
199	漫画本は捨てないでください。	Don't throw out the comic books.
200	それらは、多少の価値があります。	They're worth something.

Day 6　チェックテスト

ふさわしい語句の意味を選ぼう。　＜制限時間5分＞

1. believe：(A)〜を磨く　(B)〜を放っておく　(C)〜を信じる
2. certainly：(A) まっすぐ　(B) たぶん　(C) 確かに
3. slope：(A) ゆっくり　(B) 斜面　(C) ロープ
4. powder：(A) 銃　(B) 粉　(C) 爆弾
5. ski：(A) スキーをする　(B) 空　(C) 雪
6. get into：(A)〜に夢中になる　(B)〜から脱出する　(C)〜から降りる
7. do tricks：(A) ワナを仕掛ける　(B) 芸当をする　(C) 旅に出る
8. like that：(A) あのような　(B) それらが好き　(C) そのような
9. Sure.：(A) いいえ　(B) もちろん　(C) たぶん
10. marketing：(A) 販売促進活動　(B) 生産活動　(C) 消費

11. experience：(A)〜を実施する　(B)〜に値段を付ける
    　　　　　　(C)〜を経験する
12. unlike：(A) 嫌う　(B)〜とは異なって　(C) 好きなもの
13. horse racetrack：(A) 馬の背中　(B) 馬舎　(C) 競馬場
14. first of all：(A) まず始めに　(B) フェスティバル　(C) ものすごく早く
15. dress code：(A) ドレスの結びヒモ　(B) 服装規定　(C) コード進行
16. strictly：(A) くっついて　(B) 攻撃的に　(C) 絶対に
17. dress up：(A) 叱り飛ばす　(B) めかし込む　(C) 服をしまう
18. fashionable：(A) 流行の　(B) 融合可能な　(C) フィクションの
19. sport：(A) 走る　(B)〜を上品に着こなす　(C)〜を考える
20. stylish：(A) スタイリスト　(B) おしゃれな　(C) 盗まれやすい

21. in line：(A) 列に並んで　(B) 電話がつながって　(C) 割り込んで
22. point out：(A) ポイントがずれている　(B) その点について外す
    　　　　　(C)〜を指摘する
23. back there：(A) 後方のそこ　(B) 昔　(C) 裏側
24. to the left：(A) 残されて　(B) 左側に　(C) 左から
25. register：(A) 冷蔵庫　(B) レジ　(C) 支払い

26. sign：(A) 罪　(B) 細い　(C) 標示
27. behind：(A) 〜のうしろに　(B) 〜の下に　(C) 〜の向こう側に
28. cashier：(A) 両替所　(B) レジ　(C) レジ係
29. whatever：(A) 何でも　(B) 一体　(C) いつまでも
30. agree to：(A) 〜に接触する　(B) 〜に同意する　(C) 〜に反対する

31. across the board：(A) 板を渡る　(B) 全般にわたって
　　　　　　　　　　　(C) 板に沿って
32. sitcom：(A) ホームコメディ　(B) くつろぐ　(C) 映画館
33. purchase：(A) 在庫　(B) 販売　(C) 購入
34. way：(A) 絶対的に　(B) はるかに　(C) わずかに
35. revolution：(A) 革命　(B) 後退　(C) 前進
36. regular：(A) いつもの　(B) 変わった　(C) すばらしい
37. lazy：(A) 怠慢な　(B) 気の狂った　(C) 夢中の
38. absence：(A) 自信　(B) 常識　(C) 不在
39. back to back：(A) 最後の最後まで　(B) 連続して　(C) 繰り返し
40. leisure：(A) 趣味　(B) 余暇　(C) 娯楽

41. junk：(A) 私物　(B) 宝物　(C) ガラクタ
42. go through：(A) 〜を終わらせる　(B) 〜をくぐり抜ける
　　　　　　　　(C) 〜へ急いで行く
43. drawer：(A) 画家　(B) 引出し　(C) 運送
44. toss out：(A) 〜を手渡す　(B) 〜を押し出す　(C) 〜を放り出す
45. have seen better days：(A) 使い古された　(B) 古き良き時代
　　　　　　　　　　　　　(C) 久しぶり
46. decide：(A) 〜を決定する　(B) 〜を切り離す　(C) 〜の位置を変える
47. pile：(A) 新聞　(B) 小包　(C) 積み重ね
48. throw out：(A) 外側から　(B) 〜を捨てる　(C) 外に投げる
49. worth：(A) 〜の価値がある　(B) 何か話す　(C) 他の言い方
50. rather than：(A) 〜より大きい　(B) 〜よりむずかしい
　　　　　　　　(C) 〜よりむしろ

チェックテスト解答

1. **(C)**	2. **(C)**	3. **(B)**	4. **(B)**	5. **(A)**
6. **(A)**	7. **(B)**	8. **(C)**	9. **(B)**	10. **(A)**
11. **(C)**	12. **(B)**	13. **(C)**	14. **(A)**	15. **(B)**
16. **(C)**	17. **(B)**	18. **(A)**	19. **(B)**	20. **(B)**
21. **(A)**	22. **(C)**	23. **(A)**	24. **(B)**	25. **(B)**
26. **(C)**	27. **(A)**	28. **(C)**	29. **(A)**	30. **(B)**
31. **(B)**	32. **(A)**	33. **(C)**	34. **(B)**	35. **(A)**
36. **(A)**	37. **(A)**	38. **(C)**	39. **(B)**	40. **(B)**
41. **(C)**	42. **(A)**	43. **(B)**	44. **(C)**	45. **(A)**
46. **(A)**	47. **(C)**	48. **(B)**	49. **(A)**	50. **(C)**

＜ワンポイント＞

　第4週のトレーニング、お疲れさまでした。それでは、最後の仕上げとして、第6章で問題形式を最終確認しましょう。本番のTOEICテストでは、この1カ月間の成果が試されるわけですが、「これだけがんばったんだから、絶対に失敗はできない」という気負いは禁物です。

　TOEICテストは、470点クリアをめざされるみなさんから、900点以上をめざす方までの英語運用能力を一度に測定します。ですから、とてもやさしい問題もあれば、むずかしい問題もあります。第1章で確認した重点パート（Part 2, Part 5, Part 7のシングルパッセージ）では3問に2問の正答が目標、それ以外のパートは2問に1問わかればOKぐらいの「リラックスした気持ち」で臨みましょう。

　こう考えて、リスニングでは、聞き逃した問題をいつまでも引きずることなく、次の問題に集中する。リーディングも、むずかしい問題はあっさり捨てて、次の問題に進む。これが実は、スピード対応能力を測定するTOEICテストで実力を発揮するコツなのです。

第 6 章

最終チェック

第 6 章の使い方

TOEIC® テストの問題形式を確認する 25 問の練習問題（約 15 分）です。第 2 章～第 5 章でトレーニングしたあと、TOEIC® テスト受験直前に、問題形式の最終確認と準備に活用しましょう。

Part 1（写真描写問題）

写真を見ながら放送を聞いて、ABCD の英文から写真を適切に描写しているものを選び、答えをマークします。

1.

Ⓐ Ⓑ Ⓒ Ⓓ

2.

Ⓐ Ⓑ Ⓒ Ⓓ

＜ワンポイント＞

　Part 1 では、**人や物の状態を表わす表現**を聞き取れるかどうかが試されます。写真の人や物の状態に注意して聞きましょう。Part 1 は、**70%（10問中7問）の正答**をめざしましょう。

158

Part 2 (応答問題)

問いかけと、それに対する応答 ABC を聞いて、応答としてふさわしいものを選び、答えをマークします。

3. Mark your answer on your answer sheet.

(A) (B) (C)

4. Mark your answer on your answer sheet.

(A) (B) (C)

5. Mark your answer on your answer sheet.

(A) (B) (C)

＜ワンポイント＞
　Part 2 では、**問いかけの目的(情報収集、確認)** が理解できているかどうかが試されます。最初に流れる問いかけ文に集中して聞きましょう。Part 2 は、470 点突破の重点パートです。**60%（30 問中 18 問）の正答** をめざしましょう。

Part 3（会話問題）

2人の会話を聞いて、印刷された設問（3問）を解き、答えをマークします。

6. Which of the following does the dialogue make clear?
    (A) How long the people will be gone
    (B) Where the people are going
    (C) Whom the people plan to meet
    (D) Whether the people have traveled before

    Ⓐ Ⓑ Ⓒ Ⓓ

7. What is one thing the woman is worried about?
    (A) Money
    (B) The weather
    (C) Getting lost
    (D) Becoming tired

    Ⓐ Ⓑ Ⓒ Ⓓ

8. Where does the man think his boots are?
    (A) In the trailer
    (B) On the roof rack
    (C) In the car
    (D) Inside his suitcase

    Ⓐ Ⓑ Ⓒ Ⓓ

＜ワンポイント＞

　放送が流れる前に、設問に目を通しておくと、設問の答えを探しながら聞くことができます。470点突破には、**(勘も含めて) 40%（30問中12問）の正答で十分ですから、最低1つだけでも目を通しておく**と余裕を持って会話を聞くことができます。なお、設問は、Who（誰が）, Where（どこで）, When（いつ）で始まるものが比較的やさしい問題です。

Part 4（説明文問題） CD 89

スピーチなどを聞いて、印刷された設問（3問）を解き、答えをマークします。

9. What is the speaker describing?
   (A) An air purifier
   (B) An automobile
   (C) A musical instrument
   (D) A computer

   Ⓐ Ⓑ Ⓒ Ⓓ

10. Which of the following best describes the speaker?
    (A) Worried
    (B) Humorous
    (C) Angry
    (D) Enthusiastic

    Ⓐ Ⓑ Ⓒ Ⓓ

11. What is the advantage of the Supra 4000's features described by the speaker?
    (A) They help to provide the best safety.
    (B) They are more convenient to install.
    (C) They are larger than those in competitors' models.
    (D) They operate in close connection with the aerodynamic design.

    Ⓐ Ⓑ Ⓒ Ⓓ

＜ワンポイント＞
　Part 3 同様に、放送が流れる前に、設問に目を通しておくと、設問の答えを探すように聞くことができます。470点突破には、**勘も含めて40％（30問中12問）の正答**で十分ですから、**最低1つの設問に目を通しておく**と余裕を持って会話を聞くことができます。なお、設問は、Who（誰が）、Where（どこで）、When（いつ）で始まるものが比較的やさしい問題です。

Part 5（短文穴埋め問題）　＜制限時間1分30秒＞

空欄部を埋める語句を選びセンテンスを完成させ、答えをマークします。

12. Her mother, as well as her children, _____ in the shopping center.
    (A) was
    (B) have been
    (C) being
    (D) were

    Ⓐ　Ⓑ　Ⓒ　Ⓓ

13. With the toll-free number, information about public services is available _____ having to pay for a phone call.
    (A) either
    (B) nor
    (C) without
    (D) yet

    Ⓐ　Ⓑ　Ⓒ　Ⓓ

14. Under no _____ should he meet Mr. Smith again.
    (A) circumstance
    (B) circumstances
    (C) environment
    (D) environments

    Ⓐ　Ⓑ　Ⓒ　Ⓓ

＜ワンポイント＞

Part 5 では、基本的な語彙・文法を使用できるかが試されます。出題は、**単語の意味の違いを問う問題が 1/3、熟語などの慣用表現が 1/3、基本的な文法が 1/3**（主語と動詞の単数・複数の一致、時制、受動態など）です。470 点突破には、**60%（40 問中 24 問）の正答**が目標です。時間をかけすぎると、Part 7（読解問題）を解く時間が不足してしまいます。選択肢を一見して、わかりそうにない問題（単語の意味の違いなど）で時間をかけないようにしましょう。

Part 6（長文穴埋め問題） ＜制限時間1分30秒＞

3カ所の空欄部を埋める語句を選び文書を完成させ、答えをマークします。

Questions 15–17 refer to the following notice.

Friends of Maryville Animal Services is a nonprofit organization dedicated to _____ the Maryville animal facility.

    15. (A) be helping
        (B) help
        (C) helping
        (D) be of help

The organization is now raising funds to expand the facility, built almost a quarter of _____ century ago. In addition, with

    16. (A) the
        (B) a
        (C) one
        (D) some

winter _____, intersection the group is collecting items like

    17. (A) just around the corner
        (B) right up the street
        (C) just through the
        (D) right over the hill

old (but clean) blankets and carpets to line pens of the current facility.

＜ワンポイント＞

　Part 6では、よりライティングに近い形で、基本的な語彙・文法を正しく使用できるかどうかが試されますが、出題の内容はPart 5とほぼ同じです。470点突破には、**50％（12問中6問）の正答**が目標です。

Part 7（読解問題－シングルパッセージ）　＜制限時間3分＞

1つの英文を読んで、設問を解いて、答えをマークします。

Questions 18–20 refer to the following memo.

To: All Staff
Re.: Restroom remodeling

Please be informed that all restrooms in the building are undergoing remodeling. This will be done with as little inconvenience as possible. Please make sure all staff members know when the closures will occur on their floor.

Nov. 5-8	1st and 7th floors
Nov. 13-16	2nd and 6th floors
Nov. 20-22	3rd and 5th floors
Nov. 29-30	4th floor

Also please make sure you direct customers looking for the restrooms to the floor above or below you, as appropriate. We wish to make customers feel it is still business as usual and do not want to inconvenience them, either.

---

18. Which restrooms will be closed for the shortest time?
    (A) Those on the 1st floor
    (B) Those on the 2nd floor
    (C) Those on the 3rd floor
    (D) Those on the 4th floor

19. For whom was the memo written?
    (A) Company employees
    (B) Company managers
    (C) The building's cleaning personnel
    (D) Customers unfamiliar with the building

20. What additional task does the memo ask of its readers?
    (A) To take customers to restrooms on different floors
    (B) To help out with the remodeling of the restrooms
    (C) To familiarize themselves with a temporary schedule
    (D) To explain to customers that they must put up with some inconvenience

<ワンポイント>
英文を読む前に、**問題の導入文を見ると**（Questions 18–20 refer to the following **memo**.）、どんな種類の英文かがわかります。

> ad →広告（advertisement の省略）、memo →社内連絡文書（ある組織内でやり取りしている文書）、notice →お知らせ（社外など組織外の人に向けた文書）、review →批評（何かに対する評価のコメント）など。

次に、英文のタイトルや最初の数行（To: All Staff　Re.: Restroom remodeling）を読んで、**何のために書かれた英文か**を把握します。続いて、**設問を読んで、その答えを探すように英文を読む**と、読解にかかる時間を短縮できます。なお、知らない単語の意味を考えても時間の無駄ですから、知らない単語は無視して、わかる単語だけから推測することが大事です。Part 7（シングルパッセージ）は、470点突破の重点パートです。**60%（28問中17問）の正答**をめざしましょう。

Part 7（読解問題－ダブルパッセージ） ＜制限時間５分＞

２つの英文を読んで、設問（５問）を解いて、答えをマークします。

Questions 21-25 refer to the following memo and table.

The Flex Plan has numerous options including extended dental, medical and life insurance coverage. These options are available to full- and part-time employees although part-time employees cannot choose Option A or B until after completing 2,000 hours of employment.

If you meet that requirement, you will be enrolled in Option A unless you notify our insurers, Great Star Life. Please fill out the online application and registration form, or you may complete the form by hand and give it to your manager at your branch store.

A more detailed coverage guide as well as your insurance card (to be presented when using any medical or dental services) will be mailed to you within six weeks of your application being received.

Type	Item	OPTION A coverage (includes spouse and children)	OPTION B coverage (includes spouse)	OPTION C coverage (includes only the employee)
Medical	Private room	80%	75%	65%
	Prescriptions	80%	75%	65%
	Emergency travel	100%	90%	80%
	Vision	Exams—100% Eyewear—100%	Exams—100% Eyewear—85%	Exams—100% Eyewear—80%
Dental	Preventative/ diagnostic	80%, no max.	70%, no max.	60%, no max.
	Crowns, dentures, bridgework	60%, $1,000/yr.	60%, $1,000/yr.	No coverage

21. How does an employee get an insurance card?
    (A) By going to the company health office
    (B) By requesting it from his or her personal physician
    (C) By filling out an application
    (D) By visiting Great Star Life's office in person

22. After 2,000 hours of employment, what is a part-time employee given?
    (A) A choice about insurance coverage
    (B) The right to apply for insurance
    (C) A personal interview with a doctor or dentist
    (D) The possibility of signing up with Great Star Life

23. Unless the employee notifies the company otherwise, what percentage of his or her prescriptions will be covered by Great Star Life?
    (A) 65%   (B) 70%   (C) 75%   (D) 80%

24. Which of the following is guaranteed to a person who accepts the terms of the coverage being offered to eligible employees?
    (A) 70% of costs for bridgework for a husband, wife, or child
    (B) 75% of costs for a private room for a husband or wife
    (C) 80% of costs of preventative dental care for a husband or wife
    (D) 80% of costs for emergency travel for a husband, wife, or child

25. For options A, B and C, for which of these items is coverage the same?
    (A) Prescriptions
    (B) Eye exams
    (C) Crowns and bridgework
    (D) Emergency travel

<ワンポイント>
　470点突破には、**勘も含めて35％（20問中7問）の正答**で十分ですから、4セット（各5問）からやさしそうな問題を選んで、確実に解きましょう。

解答

Part 1

1. Look at the picture marked number 1. 1番の写真を見なさい。
   (A) The demonstrators look angry.
      デモの参加者は、怒っているようだ。
   (B) An accident has just occurred.
      ちょうど事故が起きたところだ。
   (C) A parade is going by.
      パレードが通り過ぎていく。
   (D) The two women are cheering for the team.
      2人の女性は、チームを応援している。

正解：**(C)**
解説：(A) look angry「怒っているようだ」。(B) has just occurred「ちょうど起きたところ」。(C) go by「通り過ぎる」。(D) cheer for「〜を声援する」。

2. Look at the picture marked number 2. 2番の写真を見なさい。
   (A) The bookcase is nearly empty.
      本箱は、ほとんど空っぽだ。
   (B) One book is on its side.
      1冊の本が、横向きになっている。
   (C) All of the books are just alike.
      すべての本は、同じように見える。
   (D) The bookcase is neat and tidy.
      本箱は、整然と整理されている。

正解：**(B)**
解説：(A) nearly empty「ほぼ空っぽ」。(B) on its side「横になっている」。(C) alike「似ている」。(D) neat and tidy「整然と整理されている」。

Part 2

3. Did Mr. Suzuki leave a message? 鈴木氏は、伝言を残しましたか？
   (A) Here it is. はい、これです。
   (B) He hasn't left yet. 彼は、まだいます。
   (C) I'm sure he will. 彼は、そうするはずです。

正解：**(A)**
解説：問いかけ文は、「伝言を残したか」を尋ねる疑問文。「はい、これです」と応えている（A）が正解。（B）left：leave「出発する」の過去分詞。

4. How about another helping? お代わりいかがですか？
   (A) OK, what would you like me to do? はい、どうしてほしいですか？
   (B) I don't need any help now. 今は、手助けはいりません。
   (C) Thanks, but I'm full. ありがとう、でも満腹です。

正解：**(C)**
解説：How about ～？は、「～はいかがですか？」。helping「（飲食物の）お代わり」。「満腹です」と応えている（C）が正解。（B）の help は「手助け」。

5. What line of business are you in? どんな仕事をしていますか？
   (A) I'm an engineer. エンジニアです。
   (B) I take a subway to work. 通勤には、地下鉄を使います。
   (C) Yes, I'm in line. はい、並んでいます。

正解：**(A)**
解説：問いかけ文は、「職業」を尋ねる疑問文。「エンジニア」と応えている（A）が正解。（C）の line は「列」。

Part 3

放送文

Questions 6–8 refer to the following conversation.

M: Do we have everything? Flashlight, sleeping bags, stove, Swiss knife, raingear, tarp, tent, poles . . . Did we forget anything?
W: Looks like everything is here. Oh, did you remember to throw your hiking boots in the trunk?
M: I think I did. How about our bikes? Is the roof rack sturdy enough or should we put them in the trailer?
W: In the trailer is better just in case it rains on the way there. We also should buy some more provisions. I don't think we have enough water or canned food for the two weeks.

問題6–8は、次の会話に関するものです。

M: すべて持ったかな？ 懐中電灯、寝袋、ガスコンロ、十徳ナイフ、雨具、防水シート、テント、支柱……何か忘れてるかな？
W: 全部あるようよ。あ、あなたのハイキングブーツを忘れずにトランクに入れた？
M: 入れたと思うよ。われわれの自転車は？ 車のルーフ・ラックは弱くはないかな、それともトレーラーに入れたほうがいいかな。
W: トレーラーのほうがいいわ、途中で雨が降るといけないから。それにもう少し食料品を買ったほうがいいわ。水や缶詰が2週間分には足りないと思う。

語句

stove「(料理用) コンロ」。**Swiss (army) knife**「十徳ナイフ」。**raingear**「雨具」。**tarp**「防水シート」。**remember to + 動詞**「忘れずに～する」。**throw**「～を投げ入れる」。**sturdy**「頑丈な」。**just in case**「万一の場合に備えて」。**on the way**「途中で」。**provisions**「保存食品」。**canned food**「缶詰」。

最終チェック

設問

6. この会話で明らかなのは、次のどれですか？
    (A) 彼らがどれくらいのあいだ留守にするか
    (B) 彼らがどこへ行くか
    (C) 彼らが誰に会うか
    (D) 彼らが以前に旅行をしたことがあるか

正解：**(A)**

ヒント：I don't think we have enough water or canned food for the two weeks.

7. 女性が心配なことの１つは、何ですか？
    (A) お金
    (B) 天候
    (C) 道に迷うこと
    (D) 疲れること

正解：**(B)**

ヒント：In the trailer is better just in case it rains on the way there.

8. 男性は、自分のブーツがどこにあると思っていますか？
    (A) トレーラーの中
    (B) ルーフ・ラックの上
    (C) 車の中
    (D) 彼のスーツケースの中

正解：**(C)**

ヒント：女性の Oh, did you remember to throw your hiking boots in the trunk? と、男性の I think I did.

Part 4

放送文

Questions 9–11 refer to the following presentation.
Speaking on behalf of everyone on our team, it is with great honor / that I unveil the final model. Yes, ladies and gentlemen, this is the new Supra 4000. As you'll notice, it has a sleek and aerodynamic design, with all the latest features. There's a Starboard GPS system / that comes as standard equipment / with all vehicles / in the 4000 line. The MP3-compatible surround-sound stereo system is state-of-the-art. Both front and side airbags / as well as reinforced door panels and antilock brakes / make this the safest ride on the road. Add to this / the fuel savings from driving a hybrid, and the Supra 4000 is the car of the future—today!

問題9–11は、次のプレゼンテーションに関するものです。
(※日本語訳は、英語の原文の順序どおりに記してあります。)
わがグループを代表して、大変光栄に思います / 最新モデルを発表することを。そうです、みなさん、これが新しいスープラ4000です。みなさんお気づきのように、流線型で空気力学を活かしたデザインになっています、最新の機能を備えた。スターボードGPSが付いています / 標準装備として / 全車両に / 4000シリーズには。MP3対応のサラウンドサウンド・ステレオ・システムは最新式です。前部およびサイドエアバッグ / さらに強化ドアパネルとアンチロック付きブレーキで / 走行の安全は万全です。さらに / ハイブリッド走行で燃費の節約、スープラ4000は未来の車です、今日の！

語句
on behalf of「〜を代表して」。**unveil**「〜を発表する」。**the final model**「最新モデル」。**sleek**「流線型の」。**aerodynamic**「空気力学を応用した」。**the latest features**「最新の機能」。**compatible**「互換性のある」。**surround-sound**「音が四方からくる感じを与える立体音再生の」。**state-of-the-art**「最先端の」。**reinforce**「〜を強化する」。**antilock brake**「急ブレーキをかけてもタイヤがロックしないブレーキ」。**the safest ride on the road**「路上でもっとも安全な走行」。

設問

9. 話し手は、何を説明していますか？
   - (A) 空気清浄機
   - (B) 自動車
   - (C) 楽器
   - (D) コンピュータ

正解：**(B)**

ヒント：Supra 4000 is the car of the future

10. 話し手をもっともよく表わしているのは、次のどれですか？
    - (A) 不安な
    - (B) ユーモアに富んだ
    - (C) 怒った
    - (D) 熱心な

正解：**(D)**

ヒント：商品の発表という内容から。

11. 話し手の説明によるスープラ 4000 の利点は、何ですか？
    - (A) 最高の安全を提供する。
    - (B) 取り付けが容易。
    - (C) 競合他社のものより大きい。
    - (D) 空力設計と連動して機能する。

正解：**(A)**

ヒント：Both front and side airbags as well as reinforced door panels and antilock brakes make this the safest ride on the road. なお、空気力学を活かしたデザイン（aerodynamic design）について述べられてはいるが、車の機能と連動しているかどうかは述べられていないので、(D) は不可。

Part 5

12. 彼女の子供たちだけでなく、母親もショッピングセンターにいた。

正解：**(A)**
解説：, as well as her children, は挿入句。主語は、あくまで Her mother（単数形）。したがって、was（3人称単数形）を選ぶ。as well as は、「〜だけでなく」。
例文：Her mother, as well as her children, was in the shopping center.
彼女の子供たちだけでなく、母親もショッピングセンターにいた。

13. フリーダイアルなら、電話料金を払わずに公共サービスの情報が入手できる。

正解：**(C)**
解説：having 以下は名詞句なので、前置詞 without を選び、without having to + 動詞「〜する必要なしに」を完成させる。
例文：Information is available without having to pay for a phone call.
電話料金を払わずに、情報が入手できます。

14. どんなことがあっても、彼はスミス氏に2度と会わないだろう。

正解：**(B)**
解説：文意から、under no circumstances「決して〜ない」を完成させる。なお、文頭に Under no circumstances がくると、主語・動詞は疑問文の語順に倒置する。
例文：Under no circumstances should he meet her.
どんなことがあっても、彼は彼女に会わないだろう。

Part 6

問題 15–17 は次のお知らせに関するものです。

> 「フレンズ・オブ・メアリービル動物サービス」は、メアリービル動物施設を支援するための非営利団体です。同団体では、現在、およそ 25 年前に建てられた施設拡張のための資金を募っております。加えて、冬を間近に控え、現在の施設の動物用囲いにしくための古い（ただし汚れていない）毛布とカーペットなどの品物を集めています。

15. 正解：**(C)**
解説：dedicate to + 名詞（相当語句）で、「〜に貢献する」。helping（動名詞）を選ぶ。
例文：It is an organization dedicated to helping the animal facility.
　　　それは、動物施設を支援するための団体です。

16. 正解：**(B)**
解説：「1 世紀の 4 分の 1」という文意から、a century を選ぶ。
例文：It was built almost a quarter of a century ago.
　　　それは、およそ 25 年前に建てられました。

17. 正解：**(A)**
解説：文意から、「すぐ間近（にきている）」を意味する慣用句 just around the corner を選ぶ。
例文：With winter just around the corner, the group is collecting items.
　　　冬を間近に控え、グループは品物を集めています。

Part 7（読解問題－シングルパッセージ）

問題 18–20 は次の社内連絡文書に関するものです。

全従業員へ
トイレ改修の件

当建物内のトイレを改修するので連絡します。できる限りご不便をおかけしないようにいたします。自分の階では、いつ閉鎖されるのか、全員が確認しておいてください。

11月 5日～ 8日　　1階と7階
11月13日～16日　　2階と6階
11月20日～22日　　3階と5階
11月29日～30日　　4階

また、トイレを探している顧客を上階か下階、適切なほうへご案内してください。お客様には通常業務をしているように感じていただき、ご不便をおかけしたくはありません。

| 語句 | **be informed**「お知らせします」。**undergo**「実施する」。**remodeling**「改装」。 **with as little inconvenience as possible**「できるだけ不自由をかけずに」。**as appropriate**「適切に」。 |

最終チェック

18. どのトイレが、もっとも短期間閉鎖されますか？
    (A) 1階
    (B) 2階
    (C) 3階
    (D) 4階

正解：**(D)**
ヒント：Nov. 29-30 4th floor

19. この社内連絡文書は、誰宛に書かれたものですか？
    (A) 会社の従業員
    (B) 会社の管理職
    (C) ビル清掃係
    (D) このビルに不慣れな顧客

正解：**(A)**
ヒント：To: All Staff

20. この社内連絡文書は、読み手にどんな追加の仕事を求めていますか？
    (A) 顧客を別の階のトイレに案内する。
    (B) トイレの改装の手伝いをする。
    (C) 暫定スケジュールになじむ。
    (D) 顧客に多少の不便を我慢するよう説明する。

正解：**(C)**
ヒント：Please make sure all staff members know when the closures will occur on their floor.　なお、トイレを探している人に案内するように求めてはいるが、自分のいる階が工事中でなければ、訪問客を別の階のトイレに案内する必要はないので、(A) は不可。

Part 7 (読解問題-ダブルパッセージ)

問題 21-25 は、次の社内連絡文書と表に関するものです。

> フレックス・プランには、歯科医療、医療、生命保険までの拡大保障を含む、数多くのオプションがあります。これらのオプションは、フルタイム、パートタイムいずれの従業員も利用できますが、パートタイム従業員の場合は 2,000 時間の就業時間を超えるまでは、オプション A か B の選択はできません。
>
> 要件を満たした場合、弊社契約のグレイト・スター生命に連絡しない限り、オプション A に登録されます。オンライン上の申込み登録フォームに入力するか、手書きで書式を完成させて弊社支店の担当マネージャーに提出してもかまいません。
>
> 保障内容の詳細並びに、保険カード(病院や歯科医を利用の際に提示します)については、申込書が届いてから 6 週間以内に郵送されます。

タイプ	項目	オプションAの保障(配偶者及び子を含む)	オプションBの保障(配偶者を含む)	オプションCの保障(従業員のみ)
医療	個室	80%	75%	65%
	処方箋	80%	75%	65%
	緊急搬送	100%	90%	80%
	視力	検査―100% 眼鏡など―100%	検査―100% 眼鏡など―85%	検査―100% 眼鏡など―80%
歯科医療	予防/診断	80%、上限なし	70%、上限なし	60%、上限なし
	クラウン、義歯、ブリッジ	60%、年間 1,000 ドル	60%、年間 1,000 ドル	保障なし

> **語句** numerous「数多くの」。until「(時期)までは」。meet requirement「要件を満たす」。be enrolled「登録される」。by hand「手書きで」。within six weeks of your application being received「申込書が受領されてから 6 週間以内に」。

21. 従業員は、どのようにして保険カードを受け取りますか？
    (A) 会社の保険事務所に行く
    (B) 本人の主治医に依頼する
    (C) 登録書に入力する
    (D) グレイト・スター生命のオフィスを自分で訪問する

正答：**(C)**

ヒント：上段の文章の Please fill out the online application and registration form

22. 2,000 時間就業後、パートタイムの従業員は何が得られますか？
    (A) 保険の保障に関する選択肢
    (B) 保険に申し込む権利
    (C) 医者か歯科医との個人面談
    (D) グレイト・スター生命と契約する可能性

正答：**(A)**

ヒント：上段の文章の part-time employees cannot choose Option A or B until after completing 2,000 hours of employment

23. 従業員が会社に特に断らない限り、彼らの処方箋の何パーセントがグレイト・スター生命でカバーされますか？
    (A) 65 パーセント
    (B) 70 パーセント
    (C) 75 パーセント
    (D) 80 パーセント

正答：**(D)**

ヒント：上段の文の If you meet that requirement, you will be enrolled in Option A unless you notify our insurers, Great Star Life. と、下段の表、OPTION A の Prescriptions の 80%

24. 資格のある従業員に対して提示される保障条項に同意する人に保障されるのは、次のどれですか？
    (A) 配偶者または子供にかかるブリッジ費用の70パーセント
    (B) 配偶者の個室にかかる費用の75パーセント
    (C) 配偶者の予防歯科医療にかかる費用の80パーセント
    (D) 配偶者または子供にかかる緊急搬送費の80パーセント

正答：**(C)**

ヒント：上段の文のIf you meet that requirement, you will be enrolled in Option A unless you notify our insurersと、下段の表、OPTION A coverage（includes spouse and children）のPreventativeの80％

25. A、B、Cのオプションに関して、保障が同じ項目は、どれですか？
    (A) 処方箋　　　　　　　　(B) 視力検査
    (C) クラウンとブリッジ　　(D) 緊急搬送

正答：**(B)**

ヒント：下段の表のVision, Exams-100％

＜ワンポイント＞

　ダブルパッセージの問題は、2つの英文を読んで、5つの設問に答えることが求められます。でも、焦る必要はありません。前述のとおり、470点突破には、**勘も含めて35％（20問中7問）の正答**で十分です。4セット（各5問）の中から比較的やさしそうな問題をまずチェックして、各英文の最初の数行を読み、**それぞれ何のために書かれた英文か**を把握します。これで、設問を読んだ際に、**どちらの英文から答えを探すように読めばよいのか**がわかります。比較的やさしい問題であれば、5分で1セット（5問）が解けます。最後まで、あきらめずにがんばりましょう！

本書の第 2 章〜第 5 章は、学習者向け英字新聞『週刊 ST』（ジャパンタイムズ）に、2002 年 4 月〜2010 年 3 月までの 8 年間（400 回）にわたって掲載された「TOEIC® テスト実践トレーニング」の練習問題に加筆したものです。

●編集協力
　杉山まどか

●社内協力
　高見沢紀子・菅田晶子・小倉宏子・吉井瑠里・宮内繭子

●CD製作協力
　Peter Serafin and Xanthe Smith(Golden Angel Studio)[「語句」「指示文」ほかナレーション]
　吉田美穂(俳協)[「語句」日本語ナレーション]
　佐藤京子(東京録音)

●著者紹介

http://www.icconsul.com/

鹿野　晴夫（かの　はるお）

1964年北海道生まれ。東京都立大学工学部卒。現在、英語トレーニングのICC東京本校責任者。英語レベル別指導法のエキスパートとして、企業・大学で「英語トレーニング法」の講演・セミナーを多数担当するほか、英語教員向けに「英語トレーニングの指導法セミナー」を担当している。著書に、自らの学習経験を綴った「TOEIC®テスト300点から800点になる学習法」「TOEIC®テスト900点を突破する集中トレーニング」（以上、中経出版）をはじめとするTOEIC®テスト関連の著作が40点以上。2010年には、『TOEIC®テスト　スピーキング／ライティング問題集』（研究社、千田潤一と共著）も刊行。

TOEIC®テスト　これだけ　直前1カ月　470点クリア

初版発行	2011年4月28日	
著者	鹿野晴夫 Copyright © 2011 by ICC	
発行者	関戸雅男	**KENKYUSHA** 〈検印省略〉
発行	株式会社　研究社 〒102-8152　東京都千代田区富士見2-11-3 電話　営業 03(3288)7777(代)　編集 03(3288)7711(代) 振替　00150-9-26710 http://www.kenkyusha.co.jp	
印刷所	研究社印刷株式会社	

＊

装丁・CDデザイン	久保和正
本文レイアウト・組版	(株)インフォルム
CD編集・製作	(株)東京録音

ISBN978-4-327-43070-2 C1082

本書の全部または一部を無断で複写複製（コピー）することは、著作権法上での例外を除き禁じられています。
価格はカバーに表示してあります。

研究社の出版案内

直前1カ月は、これだけきっちり仕上げよう！

鹿野晴夫〔著〕

TOEIC® テスト これだけ 直前1カ月 350点クリア

英語が超苦手な方も、
1カ月でTOEIC®の問題形式がわかる！

A5判 並製 184頁
ISBN 978-4-327-43069-6 C1082

CD付き

TOEIC® テスト これだけ 直前1カ月 600点クリア

TOEIC®テスト直前1カ月で、
さらにスコアアップをはかりたい！

A5判 並製 184頁
ISBN 978-4-327-43071-9 C1082

CD付き

▶ TOEIC®テストのスコアを上げたい。
▶ でも、あまり時間がない。
▶ 通勤・通学の時間を有効に使いたい。

そんなみなさんのために、TOEIC®の問題形式に慣れるだけでなく、基本的な英語力のアップがはかれるように工夫しました。
『週刊ST』の人気コラムに大幅加筆して単行本化！

出版社による初のTOEIC® SWテスト実戦問題集！

TOEIC® テスト スピーキング／ライティング問題集

千田潤一・鹿野晴夫〔著〕

A5判 並製 180頁
ISBN 978-4-327-43068-9 C1082

CD付き